The Preschooler's
——————— GUIDE TO ———————
D E N V E R

BEST OUTINGS FOR KIDS UNDER 6 YEARS OLD

by Carolyn Sutton

Lil' Pardner Press
An imprint of Fire Creek Publishing Corporation
Denver, Colorado

ISBN: 0-9715543-0-7
Printed in the United States of America

Published by:
Lil' Pardner Press
An imprint of Fire Creek Publishing Corporation
3685 South Narcissus Way, Suite 500, Denver, Colorado 80237
www.firecreekpub.com

Sutton, Carolyn K., 1964-
    The Preschooler's Guide to Denver / by Carolyn Sutton
    ISBN 0-9715543-0-7
    1.   Denver—Guidebooks.   2.   Family   Recreation—Denver—
    Guidebooks. 3. Children—Travel—Denver—Guidebooks.

Cover and interior design by Dianne Nelson, Shadow Canyon Graphics

Please note: Fire Creek Publishing Corporation, Lil' Pardner Press, and the author assume no responsibility for the safety of any users of this guidebook. It is understood that taking children on field trips and visiting various sites involves a certain degree of risk and that readers of this book are liable for their own actions. Although every effort was made to provide accurate and up-to-date information, Fire Creek Publishing Corporation, Lil' Pardner Press, and the author are not responsible for erroneous information, if any, contained in this book, nor for changes in prices, hours, accessibility, and other aspects of the sites described herein.

Table of Contents

Acknowledgements

ᗰᐯᗰ

TOURING ALL OF THE DENVER AREA'S BEST PLACES FOR PRESCHOOLERS is no small task, especially when you are 1 and 3 years old. Throwing in a hefty sample of Denver's not-so-great places can make a kid pretty tired. Still, my little tigers, Jay and Andrew, tromped on, mostly in good spirits, and they were always game to see another place. I am very proud of them and am grateful for their patience and fortitude as the field trips added up. I couldn't have done this without them.

Also, many thanks to Jay's and Andrew's buddies and their moms, who offered ideas and joined us on many outings. Their honest opinions were invaluable, as were the thin lips and furrowed brows that told me when a field trip idea of mine was a real flop when it came to little kids. Without their input, this would not be a book of the best places for preschoolers. Special appreciation goes to David and Peter and their mommy, Susan; also to Jacob, Brianna, and Diane, and Grant and Diane.

The wonderful librarians in the children's library of the Denver Public Library were a joy to work with. Many thanks for their guidance and suggestions for books to enrich the field trips. Honorable mention goes to Sue at the Ross-University Hills branch, who pulled terrific titles from the great card catalogue in her head.

My friend and fellow author, Mary Taylor Young, provided tremendous inspiration and support, and I will always be grateful to her for showing me how to be a mom *and* a writer. Her suggestions were always on the money.

Finally, to Clark, my husband, partner, and soul mate. This book's for you.

PHOTO BY JOE KENT

Let's Go!

Introduction

Connecting
Points

I am not a teacher, but an awakener.
Robert Frost

IF YOU HAVE KIDS, YOU KNOW THAT PEOPLE ARE MADE FROM SCRATCH. We aren't like spaghetti sauce from a jar that you just pour out, heat up, and serve. Every part of a child is homemade, and ingredients are added slowly and laboriously, until a rich and spicy stew emerges, different every time.

You will also understand that if you are a parent, you are also a teacher. From the time you first teach your newborn how to feel soothed until you are a grandparent teaching your offspring to soothe *their* babies, the guiding never ends.

> *Every part of a child is homemade, and ingredients are added slowly and laboriously, until a rich and spicy stew emerges, different every time.*

Especially in the preschool years, teaching is less about explaining facts and more about showing how to be a person. It's about sharing how to take care of oneself, how to interact with others, and what attitude to have when times get tough. Teaching at this stage is also about showing how to process information. It is about language acquisition and dealing with abstract concepts.

∧∧∧
The way kids learn in their early years is WHAT they are learning.
∧∧∧

The way kids learn in their early years is *what* they are learning. As they acquire knowledge, they form attitudes about the process itself. They decide if learning is fun and full of wonder or painful and tension provoking.

Is This Book For You?

THIS BOOK IS FOR YOU IF YOU HAVE CHILDREN OR WORK WITH THEM and you'd like to make your job a bit easier. It's for you if you'd like to be a more effective parent and teacher. And it's for you if you'd like some help adding interest and fun to the day-in, day-out routines of working with preschoolers.

The activities in this book are tailored for preschoolers for two major reasons. The first is that these years are crucial for laying

PHOTO BY JOE KENT

the foundation for learning. The preschool years are when children are developing language skills and laying the groundwork for literacy. This is the time when their brains are set up for building vocabulary and for beginning to grasp the concepts that go with the words. It is easier for kids to learn new words and concepts in the preschool years than at any other time in their lives. Now is the time to get your kids out to experience the world.

∧∧∧
It is easier for kids to learn new words and concepts in the preschool years than at any other time in their lives.
∧∧∧

PHOTO BY JOE KENT

The other reason why this book is aimed at preschoolers is because there is nothing like it for the peewee set. Books about what to do in Denver seem better suited for school-age kids, and although the ideas can be adapted for little ones, many of the sites listed in them are flat-out inappropriate for this age group.

Thus, we have carefully chosen attractions ideal for children under 6 years old. We looked for places that are both appropriate for little ones' attention spans and practical for their caregivers.

While we included a broad variety of adventures and activities for you and your preschoolers, this list of sites is by no means complete. It just scratches the surface of all the wonderful opportunities for preschoolers. Many more out there are left to be explored. We hope you will be inspired to do that.

This book is for you if you want to develop a better relationship with your kids by building memories together. It is for you if you want to enjoy parenting and teaching more. It's a chance to feel proud that you've made learning an adventure for your little ones. A positive attitude about learning is such an important ingredient in the rich and spicy stew that your kids will eventually become.

∧∧∧
A positive attitude about learning is such an important ingredient in the rich and spicy stew that your kids will eventually become.
∧∧∧

Sticking Points

CHILDREN ATTACH NEW INFORMATION to their framework of familiar ideas and experiences. This framework of information is known as schema. The Greek root means "to hold." Our schema is the means by which we hold information to ourselves. We hold new information by attaching it to experiences or knowledge that we already have. *The broader our range of experience, the more attachment points we have, and the easier it is to learn something new.*

Imagine being faced with the task of memorizing the capital cities of the 50 U.S. states. Think of doing it with only a list of states and cities in front of you. Short-term memory might allow you to regurgitate the information for a test. However, years down the road it may be hard to retrieve the information when talking with someone who happens to work in Pierre, South Dakota.

You would tell a different story, though, if you had spent a week in Pierre. What if you had walked its streets, talked with its citizens, visited its history museum, and then stopped at its capitol building to watch its legislators at work? Years later you'd be far more likely to remember it as the capital of South Dakota. That's because you would have connected that fact to numerous other points in your body of experience—your schema.

The more you know, the easier it is to learn new information. And *experiential* knowledge is more deeply understood and has more attachment points for learning. It follows that kids' learning is best based on their experiences. New information, whether it be facts (state capitals, for instance) or a way of being (resolving differences gracefully), is related to events your child has lived.

Kids' learning is best based on their experiences.

Some might think of experiential learning as some stuffy educational theory. But it's also the most natural thing in the world. Honestly, didn't your heart race when you heard the words "field trip"? Did you have the same reaction when you heard "work sheet"? Of course not. Kids love field trips because field trips give them something they are naturally hungry for—experience!

IF YOU DO NOTHING ELSE, USE THIS BOOK as motivation to get out with your kids. Smell the smells, feel the air, see the colors, hear the sounds, touch the shapes, and taste the flavors of all different kinds of places. Thumb through these pages for ideas. Go anywhere that strikes your fancy. Just get out and see the world!

Then, with little extra effort, you can multiply the benefit of the experience. While you are exploring, talk about what you are doing. Use words to name and describe the feelings, sights, and sounds. Encourage your youngsters to learn about the place with as many of their senses as possible. If they can use motor skills (climbing, poking, lifting, tickling, drawing, etc.) during your visit, so much the better.

Next, talk of similar situations they've encountered before. Show your kids how to hook new ideas into their network of past knowledge. At a very early age your little ones will be thinking laterally, putting seemingly unrelated concepts together.

These are advanced thinking skills, indeed. Yet they come naturally to even young children who are exposed to the world around them. In the long run, it may help them to solve problems more creatively. They'll have a wealth of information for devising alternatives.

DENVER ART MUSEUM

For even added richness, coordinate your trips with meaningful events. Visit the Botanic Gardens on Earth Day and the State Capitol at election time. Create connections in as many different ways as you can.

Then try the **enrichment ideas** listed with each section as pre-learning and reinforcement activities. These lay the groundwork for the trips and help your children to anticipate what's going to happen. Pre-learning activities get kids to open up their schemas and start rummaging around in them. They bring potential attachment points to the surface. Pre-learning gets the kids jazzed for the outing.

The enrichment ideas also help to reinforce what kids have learned. When you are visiting a site, look for something inexpensive or free that your child can take home. These items, and the physical manipulation of them, can help cement the trip in your child's memory. By talking about the memento and the experience, your child will build valuable verbal skills and will practice thinking in abstractions. For example, a bus schedule and map will represent a bus ride with all its smells, sights, and vibrations. Hauling out the schedule a week later will reinforce the memory of the experience and make those schema points all the stickier for attaching new information as your child encounters it.

Of course, some of the best enrichment, whether before or after an outing, is reading to your kids. We've included a list of wonderful children's books, appropriate for pre-readers, to enhance their outing experiences. All of these are available through the Denver Public Library system.

The Preschooler's Guide to Denver is more than a guidebook. It is an opportunity to enrich your own as well as your child's understanding of the world. And it is a chance for you to grow closer to your kids. Use it to build the part of your relationship based on shared experiences. Then contact us and tell us what you think. We will always be open to hearing your ideas.

Bon voyage!

Chapter 1

ᐱᐱ

Animals
Abound

TELL PRESCHOOLERS THAT THEY ARE LITTLE ANIMALS and they are likely to protest loudly to the contrary. They'll assert that animals have four legs or don't talk or are covered in fur. Yet even at this tender stage, youngsters can start to grasp what they have in common with the rest of the animal kingdom.

If they can watch and experience all kinds of beasts, children can develop a deep understanding of and appreciation for animal variety and their own place in the mosaic of life on earth.

PHOTO BY JOE KENT

Enrichment Ideas:

1. On the way to your field-trip site, play the Animal Name game. Think of as many different animals as you can. If your kids get stuck, help anticipate the visit by hinting at the animals they will see. Or suggest an unusual beast to get the ball rolling in a different direction. For example, if you're stuck on farm animals, start naming insects or fish they might find at the site. On the way home, see how many different kinds of animals your kids can remember seeing.

2. Play Animals All with your kids. Get down on the floor and pretend to be different kinds of animals. Slither and hiss like a snake, pretend you're a bear and scrounge for grubs in couch-pillow logs, or nibble on carpet "grass" as if you are a pony. The wider the variety, the more fun you will have. What does it feel like to be an ant? A whale? A sea star? An earthworm? An eagle? Let your imagination loose!

3. These three excellent books can help pre-readers understand more about the animal kingdom: *Caterpillar's Wish*, by Mary Murphy, uses beautiful pictures to explore a bug's yearning to be a butterfly; *My Visit to the Aquarium*, by Aliki, is a sweeping look at the variety of water-living animals on the planet; and *Escape from the Zoo*, by Piotr and Jozef Wilkon, is an awfully fun romp for readers, little and big.

DENVER METRO CONVENTION & VISITORS BUREAU
PHOTO BY JAN BUTCHOFSKY-HOUSER

Butterfly Pavilion and Insect Center

⋀⋁⋀

DRIFTING IN FOR A LANDING, a graham-cracker-size yellow-and-black butterfly aimed for a toddler's red shirtsleeve. The little boy froze. The insect realized its mistake and wafted into nearby leaves, searching for more promising forage. The toddler, almost 2 years old, craned and ducked, trying to follow the butterfly's flight path.

PHOTO BY JOE KENI

The Butterfly Pavilion's beauty is that visitors can walk around in the exhibit itself, where mist kisses their cheeks and huge leaves drip water on their heads. The air is steamy and sweet with the smell of loamy soil and over-ripe fruit. Butterflies, moths, and skippers, like neon figures of a huge, free-form mobile, captivate toddlers and adults alike. Over 1,200 butterflies live within the walls of the pavilion, so they are abundant and easy to spot. Kids' faces are often transfixed with delight as they track the gentle, dipping shapes.

In addition to the tropical forest, the museum also offers children a chance to meet marine invertebrates in a tidal pool exhibit. Here they pet sea stars, horseshoe crabs, and sea urchins as an interpreter explains that these are animals without backbones. In another room, kids can view all kinds of insects, including honeybees in their hive. Older, calmer preschoolers are allowed to briefly hold Rosie, a friendly tarantula, who elegantly steps her way across little fingers and into the safety of her keeper's hands.

Outside, the grounds of the pavilion are planted with butterfly gardens, native wildflowers, and prairie grass. We saw one of the most spectacular butterflies there. Adjacent to the building is open space and a nature trail with interpretive signs along Big

PHOTO BY JOE KENT

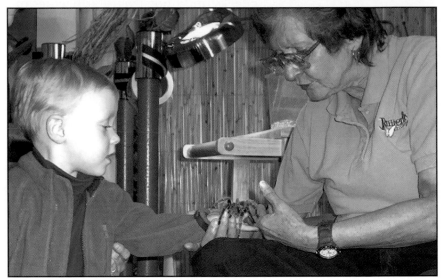

PHOTO BY MICHELE POWELL

Dry Creek. Museum members can check out backpacks with collection nets, observation jars, magnifying glasses, and guidebooks for use outside. We noticed lots of crawling creatures along the path, and the kids enjoyed getting out after being inside the museum. It was a nice conclusion to our morning with the bugs and butterflies!

Phone Number: 303/ 469- 5441

Website: www.butterflies.org

Address: 6252 West 104th Avenue, Broomfield

Directions: From I-25 and the Boulder Turnpike (Highway 36), go west to the Church Ranch Boulevard/104th Avenue exit. Go east on 104th to Westminster Boulevard and turn right. Go 1 block and turn left into the parking lot. See their website for a map.

Season: All year except Thanksgiving Day and Christmas Day

Hours: 7 days a week, 9 A.M. to 5 P.M.

Cost: $6.95 adults; $4.95 seniors; $3.95 kids 4–12 years old; 2 kids, ages 3 and under, are free with each paying adult. MasterCard, Visa, American Express, personal checks, and cash accepted.

Facilities: The Butterfly Pavilion is wheelchair and stroller accessible, and both men's and women's bathrooms have diaper decks. A snack bar offers a limited, kid-friendly menu, plus there are tables and chairs inside and outside under trees. The gift shop is full of all kinds of neat bug stuff.

Special Considerations and Notes: The busiest times at the museum are during spring break and summer vacation. In May, it hosts lots of school field trips. If you visit during those times, plan to arrive at 9 A.M. or in the late afternoon, after 3 P.M. January is the quietest time in the pavilion, and sunny days always bring out the most butterflies. At a viewing window on the west wall of the tropical forest exhibit you can watch the butterflies emerge from their chrysalises. They frequently seem to come out around 9am.

Preschoolers' Comments: "I loved holding Rosie!"

Denver Zoo

"IT'S SCWATCHY!" EXCLAIMED A LITTLE GIRL WITH BIG EYES as she drew her hand away from the fur coat of a goat. The next instant she was smiling as she stroked the soft hide of a zebu cow, just one of many African farm animals kids meet in the Kraal Animal Contact Yard at the Denver Zoo.

The Kraal is just one tool the zoo has for taking kids around the world and showing them, as intimately as possible, the marvelous variety of animal life on our planet. The zoo is in the midst of a 15-year, $125 million campaign to enhance the lives of the animals and improve the experience of its visitors. And like the Kraal, the new exhibits allow people to observe everything from frogs to gorillas in as natural an environment as possible.

DENVER ZOO
PHOTO BY RON DUNSMORE

Because of the improvements in their homes, the animals behave more naturally, and kids can understand them better. Youngsters can also see the wide variety of places that animals live, from the cold waters of the Northern Shores exhibit to the African Primate Panorama's thatched roofs.

Viewing areas are well designed for people under three feet tall, and friendly zoo volunteers in their green shirts and tan vests are often at hand to answer questions or engage a toddler in speculation.

Especially popular with the young set are the conservation carousel and the zoo train. A nice bonus: the train has been converted from diesel to clean-burning natural gas, making for a much more pleasant ride.

When You Go:
Denver Zoo

Phone Number: 303/ 376-4800
Website: www.denverzoo.org
Address: 2300 Steele Street, Denver

Directions: From I-25, take Colorado Boulevard about 5 miles north to City Park, or from I-70, take Colorado Boulevard south about 2 miles to City Park. Turn west into the park on 23rd Avenue. The main entrance is about a half-mile from Colorado Boulevard, on the left. Check the website for a map.

Season: Open every day of the year

Hours: Summer hours (April through September), 9 A.M. to 6 P.M. Winter hours (October through March), 10 A.M. to 5 P.M. Check the website for feeding and show times.

Cost: Summertime admission is $9.00 for adults; $7.00 for seniors; $5.00 for kids 4–12 years old; free for the 3 and under crowd. Wintertime admission is a dollar or so less. Parking is free. Special events, like the Wildlights in December, are extra. Check the website or call the zoo for details.

Facilities: The zoo is stroller and wheelchair accessible, and wagons are available for rent at the entrance. A few exhibits, however, require you to leave your strollers outside. Bathrooms with diaper decks are conveniently located for both moms and dads. In addition to numerous concession stands, the Hungry Elephant Café serves a nice variety of meals appealing to both kids and adults. The gift shop stocks a variety of souvenirs.

Special Considerations and Notes: Decide ahead of time which part of the zoo you would like to see most, because the whole thing in one day can be overwhelming. We like it best in winter. The crowds are thinner and many of the animals are more active. One frosty day we saw polar bears sliding and bouncing on an iceberg in their pond. Also, the zoo offers several special events throughout the year as well as preschool classes and programs. Check the zoo's website for information.

National Western Stock Show

∧∧∧

WITHOUT A MOMENT'S HESITATION, the kids dropped their coats and jumped into the great pile of dry pinto beans. Laughing, they staggered around on the slippery surface. When they fell, they buried their arms up to their armpits and then lifted their hands, fingers spread wide, raining beans down on each other. Soon their attention turned to miniature John Deere tractors, half-buried in the beans, and they began digging and pouring like pros. Before long, they left the beans for the petting zoo, where they patted a cow and watched young goats nibbling hay. Later they peered into an enclosure, laughing as ducklings paddled around in a temporary pond. For toddlers, this is the National Western Stock Show at its best.

PHOTO BY JOE KENT

The stock show is a great place for children to learn about the origins of everything, from crayons to the shoes on their feet, as well as what animals feed on, where they live, and how we train and use animals to help us work.

Mostly, the stock show is just that, a place for farmers and ranchers to show their animals, and for thousands of people to come see them. It began nearly 100 years ago and has since grown into an annual event that includes rodeos, horse shows, educational exhibits, milking demonstrations, sheep-shearing demonstrations, a petting zoo, booths for vendors, and much more. Kids have the chance to see—and smell—all kinds of beasts, and to watch many of them in action. Months after the stock show was over, my son remembered watching a competition where border collies herded sheep into a pen. He said he loved watching the "stock dogs."

Kids have the chance to see—and smell— all kinds of beasts, and to watch many of them in action.

Yet there are drawbacks for preschoolers. Primarily, the crowds can be overwhelming. Sometimes families must wait in long lines to enter the petting zoo, and it is often hard to see the exhibits because so many other little heads block the view. Also, with all of the displays, booths, and noise, little (as well as adult) nervous systems may get overloaded. We enjoyed watching horses in an outside corral as much as attending the activities inside, and it was far quieter.

Still, the stock show is a unique opportunity for kids to experience the culture and animals that are so much a part of Colorado's heritage.

WHEN YOU GO:
National Western Stock Show

Phone Number: 303/ 295-1660
Website: www.nationalwestern.com
Address: 4665 Humbolt Street, Denver

Directions: From I-25, go east on I-70 to either the Brighton Boulevard or Coliseum exits and follow the signs. Check the website for a map.

Season: Two weeks in mid-January

Hours: Open to the public, 8 A.M. to 9 P.M., although some events for stock exhibitors may start earlier.

Cost: Grounds admission is $6.00 for adults on weekdays, $8.00 on weekends and Martin Luther King Day. Grounds admission for kids ages 3–11 is $1.00 on weekdays and $2.00 on weekends and Martin Luther King Day.

Admission to special events like horse shows or the rodeo ranges from $8.00 to $18.00 and includes one-day grounds admission. Tickets can be purchased in advance on the web or by calling 1-888-551-5004. The ticket window at the stockshow complex is open from Monday through Saturday, starting the first Saturday in December. Cash, MasterCard, Visa, and American Express accepted; however, personal checks not accepted after December 31.

Parking ranges from $10.00 to $4.00 per car per day. There is free shuttle service to the Hall of Education from outlying lots.

Facilities: Both men's and women's bathrooms in the Hall of Education have diaper decks. The facilities are stroller accessible, although the most direct route to where you want to go often involves stairs. Food and souvenirs are available from numerous concessionaires.

Special Considerations and Notes: Bring lots of cash for concessions, parking, etc. Be sure to check the website or a printed schedule before you head out if you want to take in any special events like a horse show or a milking demonstration. Plan to do only one or two activities before going home. If you are staying longer, give your little one a quiet break by strolling him or her through the Coors Western Art Exhibit and looking at some stunning samples of western art.

Chapter 2

ᐱᐱ

A Kingdom in Green

PLANTS ARE LIVING ORGANISMS, JUST AS PEOPLE AND OTHER ANIMALS ARE. Because of this, we have more in common with plants than may at first meet the eye. Help your children to understand the plant kingdom by noticing similarities in different plants and animals. Emphasize those things about plants that are like your kids. (For example, plants have veins to carry fluid around inside them, and so do people!) This helps preschoolers to connect new knowledge to familiar concepts.

PHOTO BY JOE KENT

Enrichment Ideas:

1. In a tall plastic cup, mix several drops of red food coloring in water. Pull a fresh stalk of celery from a bunch, slice an inch off the bottom, and stand it up in the cup of colored water. Check the celery after a couple of hours and see if it has pulled up any of the colored water inside its "veins," or vascular bundles. If it has, slice the celery crosswise and look for the little colored dots, which are the vascular bundles in cross section. The longer you leave the celery in the colored water, the more dramatic the result. Even the edges of the celery leaves eventually become colored.

2. Go on a scavenger hunt for big and little plants. What is the biggest plant your kids can find? A lilac bush? A cottonwood tree? What is the smallest plant they can find? How about the tiny, green dots of *Elodea* in the fish tank?

3. Read *The Tiny Seed* by Eric Carle for a gentle introduction to the life cycle of a flower. *Growing Vegetable Soup* by Lois Ehlert takes young readers on a journey from planting to soup pot with colorful pictures and simple language. Both are available through the Denver Public Library system.

PHOTO BY JOE KENT

Denver Botanic Gardens

∧∧∧

HUMID AND STILL, THE AIR SEEMED THICK IN OUR LUNGS. Sweat droplets slid down our backs and legs, tickling us as they fell. We found shade beneath some foliage and paused for a moment. Suddenly I noticed that the giant leaves overhead looked exactly like a houseplant, except that they were larger than me. In the tropical conservatory of the Denver Botanic Gardens, you come face-to-face with the scale of equatorial plant life.

Here, trickling streams wind around a huge, man-made banyan tree, and the water pools under its leaves to shelter tropical fish. An elevator within the tree lets visitors take strollers up for a bird's-eye view. Winding paths below drop into a (relatively) cool grotto and subtly guide visitors back to the main entrance of the conservatory. As you explore, you begin to understand with nearly all your senses what it is like in a rainforest. And you can't help but notice the wide variety of plants, elbowing each other aside for a piece of the sun.

∧∧∧
As you explore, you begin to understand with nearly all your senses what it is like in a rainforest.
∧∧∧

The Denver Botanic Gardens is home to more than 15,000 different plant species. Its 23 acres contain more than 30 gardens of the world. Seeing it all is a daunting task with preschoolers, so study the map and visitor guide when you arrive to choose the spots that will appeal to you the most. Our little ones enjoyed the children's garden thoroughly, but the tropical rainforest in the conservatory remained their all-out favorite.

∧∧∧
The Denver Botanic Gardens is home to more than 15,000 different plant species.
∧∧∧

The Botanic Gardens rents "discovery backpacks" to school-teachers and chaperones during the week and to families on the weekends. They are designed to extend classroom learning in a hands-on environment. We tried the "family fun science pack," which is billed for all ages, but felt it was a little too structured for our 3-year-old. You can rent the packs for $3.00 at the information desk. Call 720/ 865-3577 to reserve them.

The best thing about the Denver Botanic Gardens is that it provides a place for the kids to steer their own learning in a relaxed setting with plenty of room to run and explore.

The best thing about the Denver Botanic Gardens is that it provides a place for the kids to steer their own learning in a relaxed setting with plenty of room to run and explore. They can't help but notice the plants and the different habitats, asking questions as they go. They'll never know they are practicing two key learning skills: observation of their world and a keen curiosity about what they see.

When You Go:
Denver Botanic Gardens

Phone Number: 303/ 331-4000
Website: www.botanicgardens.org
Address: 1005 York Street, Denver
Directions: From I-25, take the 6th Avenue Freeway east to Josephine Street. Turn north on Josephine and go 3½ blocks; look for the parking lot on the left. The parking lot is between Josephine and York streets. Cross York, to the west of the parking lot, and see the main entrance just north of 9th Avenue.
Season: All year except Thanksgiving and Christmas Day
Hours: Winter hours (October through April), 9 A.M. to 5 P.M. daily. Summer hours (May through September), 9 A.M. to 8 P.M., Saturday through Tuesday; and 9 A.M. to 5 P.M., Wednesday through Friday.

Cost: Winter admission is $5.50 for adults, $3.50 for seniors, and $3.00 for students and kids ages 6–15. Kids 5 and younger are free. Summer admission to the Denver Botanic Gardens is $6.50 for adults, $4.50 for seniors, $4.00 for students and kids ages 6–15. Kids 5 years old and under are free. Members receive free admission. Parking is free.

Facilities: Bathrooms for both men and women have diaper decks. Most indoor and outdoor facilities are wheelchair and stroller accessible; pick up a visitor guide with accessibility routes at the main entrance. Arrangements can be made for hearing and visually impaired visitors. During warmer months, food is available in outdoor dining pavilions. A gift shop offers a beautiful array of garden-related toys, games, books, soaps, clothing, and other gift items.

Special Considerations and Notes: The gardens host lots of curving paths that wind through foliage, making it easy for children to get lost. Keep careful track of them. Also, the paths in the children's garden are not very hospitable to strollers. A backpack carrier would work better for little ones too tired to walk.

For pre-kindergarten school groups, the Botanic Gardens offers the Sprouts Program, a hands-on gardening program geared for younger kids. It is offered in April, May, June, and September. One chaperone is required for every 8 children, with a maximum of 50 kids per school group. Call 720/ 865-3577 for details.

∧∧∧
Kids can't help but notice the plants and the different habitats, asking questions as they go. They'll never know they are practicing two key learning skills: observation of their world and a keen curiosity about what they see.
∧∧∧

Hudson Gardens

⋀⋀

A MEANDERING PATH LEADS YOU PAST CREAMY-SMOOTH SCULPTURES and through a rock garden spotted with blue, red, and yellow plumes of dryland plants. Around a bend, beneath the speckled shade of massive cottonwood trees, lies a pile of boulders. And then it appears—a passageway through the pile of rocks just big enough for preschoolers. This is Hudson Garden's hobbit hole, one of our kids' favorite spots in the whole city.

After the kids are finished climbing on and crawling through the hobbit hole, they can wander to a wooden deck built into a wetland. It is a perfect place to linger in the shade and listen to frogs chatting with one another across the water. Or, stroll to the larger main pond and watch for large grass carp swimming just beneath the surface. If you are lucky, you might see a blue heron hunting along the shore for any remaining koi fish. Walk around to the lake's western shore and see dozens of tadpoles swimming in the warm, shallow waters.

⋀⋀

And then it appears—a passageway through a pile of rocks just big enough for preschoolers. This is Hudson Garden's hobbit hole, one of our kids' favorite spots in the whole city.

⋀⋀

With all this wildlife, you might think Hudson Gardens is a nature center. But with 16 distinct, artistically designed and cultivated areas, these are beautiful show gardens. Bordering the South Platte River, Hudson Gardens covers 30 acres and displays thousands of flowers, trees, and other plants that grow in Colorado's

⋀⋀

Bordering the South Platte River, Hudson Gardens covers 30 acres and displays thousands of flowers, trees, and other plants that grow in Colorado's dry climate.

⋀⋀

dry climate. Sites include cascading streams, conifer groves, wild-flower meadows, and a secret garden. Mountain views might surprise you throughout the grounds. It's a wonderful place where native plants and animals abound.

Two other gardens are of particular interest to kids under 6 years old. The garden railroad features model trains that run past waterfalls and across trestles, covering over 500 feet of track. Plants adorning the railroad match the miniature scale of the trains. In the fragrance garden, visitors are encouraged to touch the plants, helping to release the sometimes subtle, sometimes strong, scents of the vegetation. It is a wonderful opportunity to engage at least four of the five senses in your child's exploration.

A large lawn offers a terrific space for little ones to run around and burn off energy. This doubles as a concert space on certain summer evenings. The gardens also host several special programs throughout the year, including a Mother's Day brunch, an old-fashioned 4th of July, ghosts in the gardens, and supper with Santa.

Park benches and picnic tables are scattered across the grounds, creating perfect snack and picnic-lunch spots. Combined with shade trees, abundant flowers, and open spaces, they make for a relaxing day with your preschoolers in the gardens.

When You Go:
Hudson Gardens

Phone Number: 303/ 797-8565
Website: www.hudsongardens.org
Address: 6115 South Santa Fe Drive, Littleton
Directions: From I-25, take Santa Fe Drive south just past Bowles Avenue in Littleton. Look for the entrance on the west side of the road, just after passing Arapahoe Community College on the east.
Season: Hudson Gardens is open year-round
Hours: May through September, 9 A.M. to 5 P.M.; October through April, 10 A.M. to 2 P.M.

Cost: Summer admission is $4.00 for adults, $3.00 for seniors, and $2.00 for kids 3–12 years old. Winter admission is free. Parking is free.

Facilities: Most of the gardens are wheelchair accessible, as is the log-cabin restaurant, which is only available to rent for special events. The gift shop is open April through October. Bathrooms are handicap accessible, and a changing shelf is available in the women's restroom. There is only a small snack bar (Oasis on the Platte) outside the western gates to Hudson Gardens. It offers smoothies, ice cream, and other snacks, but no substantial lunch food.

Special Considerations and Notes: Hudson Gardens are accessible from the wide, cement bike path that runs along the Platte River. Look for the Oasis on the Platte snack bar, where you can buy admission tickets and enter through a gate nearby.

Welby Gardens

∧∧∧

OUR TOUR GUIDE LEANED AGAINST THE SLIDING DOOR OF THE STEAM ROOM to push it open. Clouds billowed from the opening, and he stepped inside. Tentatively, the preschoolers followed, intimidated by the moisture and shadows within. Rows of carts lined the interior, their shelves filled with germinating seeds. This is the nursery, where baby plants are born.

Stepping through another doorway, the children were surrounded by more steam, this time so warm that they broke into a sweat almost immediately. Before they reached the exit, though, the sliding door was shut behind them, and they learned that tiny shoots grow best in the dark.

A tour through Welby Gardens is a journey through a variety of climates. Every plant type has a preference for humidity and temperature, and the greenhouse operators have it down to a science. But these growers of Hardy Boy plants are artists as well, and the tour guide has a flare for dramatics that keeps kids interested. He starts with geraniums, and the kids' first stop is in a huge sea of red blossoms.

∧∧∧
The Welby Gardens greeenhouses cover several acres, and kids get their exercise walking through them. They see tiny baby plants before they are transplanted, and they watch mature plants being loaded onto trucks, bound for garden shops and nurseries in several states.
∧∧∧

The Welby Gardens greenhouses cover several acres, and kids get their exercise walking through them. They see tiny baby plants before they are transplanted, and they watch mature plants being loaded onto trucks, bound for garden shops and nurseries in several states. They notice the spicy smell of thousands of sweet alyssum plants, and they feel the cooling breeze

when the huge greenhouse fans turn on. Our guide picked a stalk of pineapple sage for each of the children to sniff and showed them the whiskered faces of pansy blossoms.

Talk with your kids about the process, from greenhouse to garden shop to family gardens at home; children are delighted to understand the connection to their own experience. Later, after your field trip is through, plant flowers from the flats of bedding plants that you can buy at Welby Gardens. It will give your kids the chance to remember and talk about their trip—an excellent way for them to integrate their adventure with their life.

Phone Number: 303/ 288-3398

Address: 7390 North Clayton Street, Denver

Directions: From I-25, take I-76 northeast to the 74th Avenue exit (exit #8). Turn left toward Welby just after exiting and go east on Colorado 224, which is 74th Avenue. You will see the greenhouses and gardens lining the right side of the road. Look for the Welby Gardens sign on the right, and turn right (north) on Clayton Street and right again into their parking lot.

Season: Year-round, but they are closed to tours during the months of April and May (when they are too busy getting their flowers out!). Late July to early August is the best time to see the trial gardens in full bloom.

Hours: Call ahead to arrange a tour.

Cost: There is no cost for the tour; however, this is a busy wholesale greenhouse, and they appreciate it if you buy some flats of flowers to take with you for the kids to plant or if you offer a donation to compensate them for their time.

Facilities: Bathroom facilities are limited and do not have diaper decks. The greenhouses are not conducive to strollers; a backpack baby carrier is more practical. There are no facilities for eating on the premises; however, there is a retail garden shop where you can buy souvenirs of the trip.

Special Considerations and Notes: Welby Gardens is a huge commercial enterprise, and although they give excellent tours to groups of preschoolers, it is not a routine activity for them. Be conscious of their time, and be sure the kids are under control and can follow rules, both for their own safety and to protect Welby Gardens' merchandise.

Chapter 3

Rockin' and Rollin'

ROCKY CONNECTING POINTS

ROCKS ARE OUR FOUNDATION. They create homes for plants and animals. We use their parts to make all kinds of things around us, including our houses, roads, and playgrounds.

Rocks also record events that occurred long before we were here. They tell stories of ancient glaciers and volcanoes, of forests and dinosaurs and asteroids. At first they seem lifeless and still, yet rocks are constantly in motion. On our time scale, that is hard for us to imagine.

The preschool years are perfect for introducing children to geology. Their experiences at this age will help them understand abstract concepts later. Get the kids out rubbing, smelling, and climbing on rocks. Encourage them to notice different colors, sizes, shapes, and textures of rocks. Don't be afraid to use big words like "sediment" and "oxidize," as long as you demonstrate what you mean. Help your preschoolers to see how fun rocks can be!

Enrichment Ideas:

1. Start a rock collection. Get an old shoebox and collect one or two rocks from each field trip. Keep a piece of paper and a pencil in the box to record information about each rock; for example, list the color, size, shape, and weight of each rock. You don't need to use exact measurements, but if you keep a ruler in the box, this can add to the fun. Also note the place where you picked up the rock, and where the rock may have come from (a nearby slope, a roadbed, a stream bottom?). Help your youngsters to notice the differences between varieties of rocks, especially color, heaviness, and grain size.

2. Create rock formations in the sand. At the beach or in the sandbox, start building a mountain of sand, and as you pile it up, make layers of different materials. Create a layer of pinecones and a layer of sand, then a layer of big rocks, then a layer of sand, next small rocks and sand, then wood chips and sand, and so on until the pile is nearly as tall as a toddler. Fill a watering can with water and let your kids use the gentle streams to wash away the sand, revealing the building materials within the mountain. It will give them a good hands-on feeling for geological forces like erosion.

3. *Everybody Needs a Rock* by Byrd Baylor is an amiable read about a kid's relationship with a rock, while *Dinosaur Roar* by Paul and Henrietta Stickland is a playful exploration of opposites in the dinosaur world. Both are excellent pre-field-trip books. *Dinosaurs, Dinosaurs* by Byron Barton is perfect for bedtime after a day in the field or museum.

PHOTO BY JOE KENT

Red Rocks Park and Amphitheater

∧∧∧

FROM WHERE WE WERE SITTING ON THE TOP—the back row of Red Rocks Amphitheater—Susan, her son David, and baby Peter looked like brightly colored ants down on the stage. Just behind them loomed an orange rock the size of a small house. Beyond that, to the east, the land dropped away to a panorama of the Denver basin, with downtown Denver's tiny skyscrapers poking up from its middle.

Inspired by the spectacle of nearly 10,000 seats rising before her, Susan broke into song. "Twinkle, Twinkle, Little Star," sailed up to us at the top of the amphitheater, the words amplified and funneled by giant rocks on either side of the seating area. We heard her clearly from hundreds of rows above her.

We clambered down to the stage and turned to ogle up at gigantic Creation Rock and Ship Rock, flanking terrace upon terrace of concert seating. We imagined how much fun musicians would have playing in such a rugged setting, before such huge crowds.

PHOTO BY JOE KENT

Red Rocks, part of the Denver Mountain Parks system, attracts visitors from around the world. Although the park itself covers almost 640 acres, the main attraction is the amphitheater. During the off-season, and in the mornings of event days, it is a terrific romping ground for high-energy preschoolers.

However, it's a long hike back up the stairs from the stage to the parking lot. It's easy for little kids to get tired. But by taking their time and resting occasionally as they climbed, our 3-year-olds made it all the way on their own. It was great exercise and tired them out for naps!

The park is full of lunch spots, including a group picnic shelter near a geological marker just off Tunnel Road. The marker is on an overlook at the end of a short, wheelchair- and stroller-accessible gravel trail. If you eat there, be sure to bring lots of wipes—no running water is available. Nearby is a modern, well-built outhouse.

The snack bar in the trading post serves basic lunch fare at very reasonable prices. Its back deck overlooks colossal flame-colored boulders emerging from the greenery and a panoramic view of the Dakota Ridge valley. Even on a concert day we had the place to ourselves, and the kids loved looking through the rustic log railing at the beautifully landscaped yard below.

The park's trading post has a history room with pictures and artifacts about Red Rocks. Kids can see photos of the amphitheater filled with concertgoers and a display about its construction.

Enrich your visit by pulling out near the tunnel on Tunnel Road. Get out and touch the rock at the entrance of the bore and hoot into it to hear your echoes. Then, in the history room of the trading post, look for a photo of workers digging the tunnel. It shows how crews from the Civilian Conservation Corps drilled out tons of rock to make the hole. The picture is more meaningful after visiting the tunnel, and it helps kids understand its construction.

All in all, Red Rocks Park and Amphitheater is one of the most scenic field trips for preschoolers in Denver. It is also the perfect spot for kids to develop observation skills and curiosity about the geological forces within our earth.

Phone Number: 303/ 295-4000
   or 303/ 697-8935 for the trading post
Website: www.redrocksonline.com
Address: 16351 County Road 93, Morrison
Directions: Take I-70 west of C-470 to the Morrison exit (exit #259). Go southeast on Colorado State Highway 26 just over a mile and look for the entrance on the right.
Season: Open all year
Hours: 5 A.M. to 11 P.M., except on concert days when the park closes at 1:30 P.M.
Cost: There is no fee to use the park except on concert days, and then your fee will be refunded if you leave the park before the event.
Facilities: The park has a trading post with restrooms and a snack bar. You can get a map of the park and its hiking trails there. There is also a Port-o-let at the top of the amphitheater and an outhouse and group picnic area at the geological marker.
Special Considerations and Notes: The amphitheater itself was closed for construction and reopened for concerts in June 2002. A visitors center, located at the top of the amphitheater, will be open in early fall of 2002. This brand-new facility promises state-of-the-art bathrooms and should include a snack bar and interactive exhibits featuring the geology, construction, and musical history of Red Rocks Park.

Denver Museum of Nature and Science

∧∧∧

GEMS AND MINERALS HALL

STEP INTO A LONG, DIM MINING TUNNEL and begin your exploration of the Gems and Minerals Hall at the Denver Museum of Nature and Science. Heavy wooden beams support a low ceiling. Light bulbs hang overhead, strung together by a heavy, yellow extension cord. The tunnel opens to a dark, disheveled cavern, glittering as if newly coated by a blizzard of giant sugar crystals.

Miners in northern Mexico were searching for silver when they first spied the glints and shimmers of this buried fairyland. They took care to preserve the cavern, and eventually it was dug up and transported to the Denver Museum of Nature and Science. Here the grotto has been reconstructed, and visitors can see how it appeared when it was first discovered. Nearby signs explain the way such beautiful shapes were formed underground.

∧∧∧

Heavy wooden beams support a low ceiling. Light bulbs hang overhead, strung together by a heavy, yellow extension cord. The tunnel opens to a dark, disheveled cavern, glittering as if newly coated by a blizzard of giant sugar crystals.

∧∧∧

Turn a corner and stroll into the pretend-granite tunnels of the Sweet Home Mine. This replica is complete with moaning, gushing mine noises and authentic-looking veins of minerals. The rocks are looming and dark and may frighten toddlers. But just inside are beautiful secret pockets of actual blood red rhodochrosite crystals surrounded by sparkling quartz needles, and within a few feet you are back in a well-lit area with interactive exhibits for the kids to touch.

One of our favorite displays is of phosphorescent rocks. Kids can push a button that turns off the regular lights and shines an ultraviolet lamp on the minerals. This makes the minerals glow

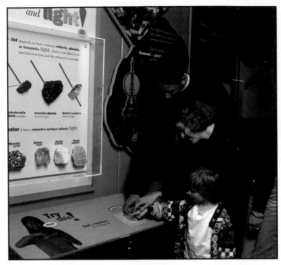

DENVER MUSEUM OF NATURE AND SCIENCE

in the dark with eerie, neon shades. Unfortunately, this display is too high for preschoolers, so adults must pick them up to help them see. One preschooler enjoyed the changing colors so much that his mom figured she had completed two full sets of weight-lifting repetitions before they moved on.

Much of the Gems and Minerals Hall is static. To a preschooler, it is just a bunch of rocks behind glass. The chemical compositions and classifications are way beyond the little ones and don't hold their interest. But the mine replica and the crystal cavern are really exciting. One boy kept running back to see those displays over and over again. I thought the field trip had been only so-so with my kids until that night when I heard my son telling his stuffed "aminals" all about the sparkly cave long after I had kissed him goodnight.

PREHISTORIC JOURNEY

WHEN YOU WALK IN THE FRONT DOORS of the Denver Museum of Nature and Science, you are welcomed by a toothy grin. A giant fossilized skeleton of *Tyrannosaurus Rex* rears up and ushers you toward the ticket counter with claws outstretched. A Wal-Mart greeter, this is not. However, he is a perfect introduction to Prehistoric Journey, the museum's collection of fossil dinosaur bones.

This outstanding assortment of skeletons includes stegosaurus, the Colorado state fossil, and diplodocus, whose neck and tail snake over almost the entire length of the room. They are

placed in lifelike poses with clues in the exhibits to help visitors understand how they lived and died. In several places, bones are displayed as they were found, jumbled in beds of rock or mud.

In other rooms, kids can experience primeval mammals and birds in their natural environments, complete with the sound of buzzing insects and footsteps crunching towards them through the underbrush. It spooks some of the preschoolers into the arms of moms and teachers, yet they are intrigued enough to linger and see what happens next.

Another favorite stop is the lab for Prehistoric Journey. Large windows and brilliant lighting allow kids to watch real paleontologists work to free dinosaur fossils from chunks of rock. They chisel away, surrounded by microscopes, chemicals, and sharp little instruments. If you are lucky, you will be able to catch someone working with his or her window open and answering questions from visitors.

DENVER MUSEUM OF NATURE AND SCIENCE

Prehistoric Journey is a great excursion for preschoolers, dinosaur fan or not.

WHEN YOU GO:
Denver Museum of Nature and Science

Phone Number: 303/ 322-7009 or 800/ 925-2250
Website: www.dmnh.org
Address: 2001 Colorado Boulevard, Denver
Directions: From I-25, take I-70 east to the Colorado Boulevard exit. Go south on Colorado Boulevard to 20th Avenue. The Denver Museum of Nature and Science is in City Park.
Season: Year-round, but the museum is closed on Christmas Day.
Hours: During the summer schedule (Labor Day through Memorial Day), the museum is open from 9:00 A.M. to 5:00 P.M. every day except Tuesday, when it is open until 7:00 P.M. During the winter, the museum is open every day from 9:00 A.M. to 5:00 P.M.

Cost: Admission to the museum is $7.00 for adults and $4.50 for children ages 3–12. The museum offers several free days each year. Check the website for a list. Members are free. Parking is free but limited on busy days.

Facilities: The museum is wheelchair accessible and stroller accessible and has large restrooms with diaper decks. There is also a snack bar with a kid-friendly dining area and a big gift shop.

DENVER MUSEUM OF NATURE AND SCIENCE

Dinosaur Ridge
Nature Center

∧∧∧

THE SUN BLAZED OVERHEAD AND INSECTS BUZZED IN THE GRASSES. Ahead of us, the plains veered sharply to a ridge jutting into the blue sky. A road snaked its way up the hillside and disappeared over the top. Along its route, blond sheets of rock appeared across the slope at uneven intervals. People clustered near the bottom of the rocks, peering up and pointing.

Soon a minibus, colorfully decorated with prehistoric reptiles, picked us up. The "vanosaurus" carried us over the ridge's crest and dropped us near the bottom on the other side. And there, next to a cement platform and interpretive signs, were the dinosaur bones, dark and shiny, imbedded in butterscotch sandstone.

This is Dinosaur Ridge, the site of several dinosaur discoveries, including stegosaurus and diplodocus, dating back as early as 1877. Walking back up the road, we came next to the "Bronto

PHOTO BY JOE KENT

Photo by Joe Kent

Bulges." These dips in the rock were made when a brontosaurus walked by. It was so heavy it actually warped the sandstone layers below its feet. The surrounding layers have since lifted up and flaked away, revealing a cross-section of footprints that appear as giant bulges.

There are 17 geological sites on the road between the visitor center and the bone site. Our walk from end to end covered 1¼ miles and took about 1½ hours. At each site, signs interpret for visitors what they are seeing. Our kids saw fossils in their original places and contemplated the dramatic uplift of the Rocky Mountains. The view from the summit was spectacular.

We visited during Dinosaur Discovery Days, a monthly summertime program. The road (State Highway 26) was closed to traffic—definitely a benefit for families with preschoolers—and guides were on hand to answer questions. Unfortunately, their audience was mostly older kids and adults and the information was too advanced for our youngsters. At the one site where we had a guide to ourselves, he did a beautiful job of explaining fossils on a level our kids could understand.

Dinosaur Discovery Days' biggest advantage is that the vanosaurus runs every 10 minutes or so. It will give you a ride to the beginning of the trail and pick you up part way back, when little feet start to drag. An even better option is to reserve a tour (call at least 3 weeks in advance) for preschoolers. You can ride with a guide in the vanosaurus, visit the most outstanding sites, and hear facts geared to the kids' interest level. It takes only about an hour.

The highlight of Dinosaur Ridge is stop number 4, a dinosaur trackway. More than 300 footprints mingle, telling chilling tales of plant- and meat-eating dinosaurs, adults and babies, and the drama of life. During tours and Dinosaur Discovery Days, kids can climb near and actually touch the footsteps of ancient beasts. It can provide a memory that will last a lifetime.

When You Go:
Dinosaur Ridge Nature Center

Phone Number: 303/ 697-DINO (3466)

Website: www.dinoridge.org

Address: 16381 West Alameda Parkway, Morrison

Directions: From I-70, take the Morrison exit (exit #259) and go south on Colorado State Highway 26 about 1⅓ miles to the junction with County Road 93. Turn left at the intersection, staying on Highway 26, and travel up and over the hogback and down the other side. You will now be on Alameda Parkway. Look for the Dinosaur Ridge Visitor Center on the left at the bottom of the hill.

If you go during Dinosaur Discovery Days, this route will be closed. Then, take I-70 to exit #259 and go *north* on U.S. 40 toward Golden. Curve around to the east on U.S. 40 where it turns into Colfax Avenue and turn south (right) on Rooney Road. Go south a little more than 2 miles to the intersection with Alameda Parkway. The visitor center will be on the left and Dinosaur Ridge is on the right. Check the website for a map.

Season: The self-guided tour, the Dinosaur Ridge Trail, is open year-round. Dinosaur Discovery Days, held one weekend a month, begin in May and continue through the summer. May and October are the busiest months for private tours. Call well over a month in advance during those times.

Hours: The visitor center and gift shop are open 9 A.M. to 4 P.M., Monday through Saturday, and 12 P.M. to 4 P.M. on Sunday. The Dinosaur Ridge Trail is along a state highway, and therefore it is open all the time.

Cost: The self-guided tour and parking are free; $2.00 per person to ride the vanosaurus during Dinosaur Discovery Days. Reserved tours are $35.00 for the first 12 people and $3.00 per person thereafter for groups larger than 12. One guide can accommodate up to 30 people.

Facilities: In addition to the Dinosaur Ridge Trail, which you can walk or drive, the visitor center has picnic tables and an outhouse, but no diaper decks or running water. Bottled drinking water is for sale in the visitor center. The gift shop has a wonderful array of souvenirs to wow even the most jaded dino-lover.

Special Considerations and Notes: The trail is along the road as it climbs over the ridge, so supervise your preschoolers carefully. Hats, sunscreen, and drinking water are absolutely necessary. During Dinosaur Discovery Days, or if you decide to walk the entire trail, strollers and backpack baby carriers are a good idea.

Interpretive sign #15 discusses "Bronto Bulges," or tracks possibly made by a brontosaurus. These tracks hang down from an overhang that is unsupported and has the potential to come crashing down, along with tons of rock. The organization is in the process of looking for funding to shore up the overhang; however, in the meantime, *do not let children crawl under the overhang.* It is possible to enjoy the bulges from the safety of the trail.

Chapter 4

ᴧᴧᴧ

Gotta Get Going

ONE OF THE HALLMARKS OF OUR CULTURE is that we tend to move things around—ourselves and our stuff. Familiarity with transport in its many different forms helps kids understand our society, our geography, our technology, our physics, and our economics.

Besides all that—or maybe because of it—many kids are fascinated by transportation. For example, my son has been to no less than 7 transportation-theme birthday parties in his 3 short years. It follows that in addition to being terrifically educational, transportation field trips are guaranteed to be a big hit with the under-6 crowd.

RTD

Enrichment Ideas:

1. Tear a variety of different transportation pictures from old maga-zines. Help older kids sort the pictures into categories. Encourage your kids to talk about:

   • the type of transportation;
   • what's being transported;
   • distances covered by different kinds of transport;
   • and how much energy it takes to move different things around.

   Then, before a field trip, pull out the pictures of the kind of trans-port you will be visiting and take them with you. See what the kids recognize in real life.

2. Children's literature abounds with wonderful books about trans-portation. Three good ones are: *Away We Go!* by Rebecca Kai Dotlich, *This Plane* by Paul Collicutt, and *Train Song* by Harriet Ziefert. And *Six Hogs on a Scooter* by Eileen Spinelli is a silly roundup of transportation options sure to get a giggle from your youngsters.

PHOTO BY JOE KENT

Colorado Railroad Museum

⋀⋀

Dong, ding! Dong, ding! The clanging of a heavy locomotive bell summoned us to the Colorado Railroad Museum, otherwise known as Heaven for Little Train Fans. The museum building is a replica of an 1880s train depot. Tickets in hand, we pushed through a swinging gate and outside to the train yard. More than 60 historic train cars and locomotives greeted us. Immediately the kids clambered up steep steps and were leaning through the window of an 1890 steam locomotive. Pulling hard on a grubby rope, they summoned the next visitors to the museum. Dong, ding! Dong, ding!

Photo by Joe Kent

Although a sign warned us that this was, in fact, a historical museum and not a playground, plenty of engines, railroad cars, and cabooses were open for visitors to climb on and explore. Our kids loved mousing around in the trainmen's cars, checking out bunks, cast-iron stoves for warming the compartments on chilly rides, and numerous cubbyholes. More than one caboose featured benches high in the cupola. The kids imagined being railroad workers watching the country go by through the windows of this lofty perch.

The ground between the trains is rough, and it isn't possible to bring a stroller to several of the cars. I was glad to have a carrier for our 9-month-old. And the picnic tables are a long way from the car, but the path to them is smooth enough to pull a wagon full of picnic gear. Park benches are strategically scattered throughout the outside railroad yard and around a miniature train run by the Denver Garden Railway Society

Inside the museum, displays of old photos, documents, and artifacts tell the history of Colorado trains since 1867. The basement holds an HO-scale model railroad complete with a mountain backdrop, mining shafts cut into the miniature hills, tunnels, towns, and an old-fashioned carnival. For a quarter, the train will run around the track for kids to watch. Unfortunately, the viewing windows are at a height perfect for adults, but kids need to be lifted up to see through them.

The museum gift shop and bookstore are full of train memorabilia, perfect for encouraging preschoolers to remember and talk about their visit.

WHEN YOU GO:
Colorado Railroad Museum

Phone Number: 303/ 279-4591 or 800/ 365-6263
Website: www.crrm.org
Address: 17155 West 44th Avenue, Golden
Directions: From I-25, take I-70 west almost to Golden. Take exit #265 and travel west on 44th Avenue past McIntyre Street. The museum is on the right (north) side of the street. Check the website for a map.

Season: Year round, but closed Thanksgiving and Christmas Day.

Hours: 9 A.M. to 5 P.M. daily, and open until 6 P.M. during June, July, and August.

Cost: $6.00 for adults, $3.00 for children under 16, and $5.00 for seniors, or families can pay $14.50 for 2 adults and their children under 16.

Facilities: The women's bathroom has a diaper deck, and it is possible to tour much of the grounds in a wheelchair or stroller. The HO-scale model railroad in the basement of the museum building is not wheelchair or stroller accessible. There is a gift shop with lots of serious train memorabilia for sale, and several picnic tables are set up on a shady lawn.

PHOTO BY JOE KENT

RTD Light Rail
and Buses

∧∧∧

As we pulled into our preschool's parking lot, my son exclaimed, "Hey! There's a circulator bus!"

Sure enough, the city bus, full of kids from the Dinosaur Room, exited the driveway and continued on its route. During the course of the morning, the "Dinosaurs" would visit a fire station, a police station, and the city council chambers. They would watch commuters get on and off at different bus stops, and I'll bet they would sing "The Wheels on the Bus."

For kids from a culture addicted to cars, it was a real adventure.

The Regional Transportation District (RTD) runs a metrowide network of city bus routes, plus other means of transport like the light-rail trains, the skyRide buses to Denver International Airport, and circulator buses like the B-Line of South Colorado Boulevard or the Link in the Denver Tech Center. Many of the

PHOTO BY JOE KENT

routes, like the light rail and the circulator buses, run so frequently that you don't even need a schedule. Just wait at a bus or train stop and within a few minutes the bus or train will be there. If you want a schedule, each bus or train carries pamphlets with its route map and schedule on it. The kids love these as souvenirs of their trip.

Our favorite routes are the 40, down Colorado Boulevard to the Denver Zoo, and the skyRide for a field trip out to Denver International Airport.

We have been known to get on the light-rail train and ride just for the fun of it. Kids also love the lofty view from bus windows and watching all the people get on and off. On days when we actually have a destination, it can be a little more work checking the schedule and then leaving in time to catch the bus, but it is more than worth it in entertainment value and the lack of parking hassle once we are there.

WHEN YOU GO:
RTD Light Rail and Buses

Phone Number: 303/ 299-6000
Website: www.rtd-denver.com
Address: Main offices: 1600 Blake Street, Denver
Directions: Check the website for a great map of all the routes in metro Denver, including light rail and skyRide. You can also call the information number to get directions on how to ride the train or buses from wherever you are to wherever you want to go.
Season: Year-round
Hours: Some routes run 24 hours a day, and others run only during the day. Check the website or schedules for times.
Cost: Fares start at $1.10 for adults for local travel and go up to $10.00 for a one-way trip to Denver International Airport for skyRide's suburban routes.
Facilities: Bus stops and train stations do not have restrooms, so encourage your little ones to go before you leave. Eating and drinking are not allowed on the buses and trains, although snacks are fine while waiting at a stop.

∧∧∧
We have been known to get on the light-rail train and ride just for the fun of it. Kids also love the lofty view from bus windows.
∧∧∧

Denver International Airport, Jeppesen Terminal

∧∧∧

JAY COULD HARDLY CONTAIN HIMSELF in the seat of the big airport bus. "There's the control tower! There's Jeppesen Terminal! Why don't we have suitcases?"

As we climbed off the bus and headed into the grand open space beneath the tentlike ceiling of the main building, a sense of freedom overcame me. What fun to explore the airport without worrying about luggage or planes to catch!

PHOTO BY JOE KENT

And the kids had a ball. They watched the baggage rumble around on the carousels and threw pennies into the fountain. They saw huge murals with brightly colored images from Colorado history. They rode escalators to balconies just below the dippy roof and looked down at crowds of travelers.

The concourses, and the underground train carrying passengers to them, are closed to people without tickets. However, the best part of DIA is its spacious atrium, which is open to all. At 900 feet by 210 feet, it offers plenty of room for working off toddler energy. When the security process slows, some areas may be congested; however, there is still plenty of room for kids.

At the north end of the terminal is a large statue of Elrey B. Jeppesen, one of aviation's most influential pioneers. It is surrounded by interesting displays about his life and work. It provided a calm place to regroup the kids before getting back on the bus and heading home.

WHEN YOU GO:
Denver International Airport, Jeppesen Terminal

Phone Number: 303/ 342-2000
Website: www.flydenver.com
Address: 8500 Peña Boulevard, Denver
Directions: From I-25, go east on I-70 or take I-225 northeast to I-70. Proceed east on I-70 to the Peña Boulevard exit. Round the curve and go north, then east on Peña Boulevard to the terminal. Watch signs for parking. Check the website for a map.
Season: Year-round
Hours: Open to the public 24 hours a day, 7 days a week
Cost: Visiting the terminal is free, but parking costs range from economy parking at $1.00 per hour (includes shuttle service), to valet parking at $9.00 for the first hour and $2.00 per hour thereafter.
Facilities: The airport is completely wheelchair and stroller accessible, and the bathrooms have convenient diaper-changing counters. There are several places to eat, as well as newsstands for picking up airport souvenirs.

∧∧∧

And the kids had a ball. They watched the baggage rumble around on the carousels and threw pennies into the fountain. They saw huge murals with brightly colored images from Colorado history. They rode escalators to balconies just below the dippy roof and looked down at crowds of travelers.

∧∧∧

Forney Museum

∧∧∧

RIGHT INSIDE THE DOOR OF THE FORNEY MUSEUM is a small model railroad display with two oval tracks traveling through a miniature village. For a quarter, kids can push a lever to make one of the trains go around and around. The farther they push the lever, the faster the train will run. The gift-shop proprietor said that at a quarter a piece, it is one of the museum's biggest money makers.

It is also one of the few interactive exhibits in the museum. A collection of elderly, rare vehicles, the museum's displays are mostly for looking at. Yellow lines on the floor and plastic chains keep visitors at a distance from the cars and trains.

The one notable exception is the Big Boy locomotive, one of the 8 remaining largest steam locomotives in the world. Kids can touch and rub the huge wheels and tanks without much fear of hurting it. Climbing on it, however, is not recommended. The iron steps of the ladders are inviting, but the rocks, railroad ties, and cement sidewalk below would make for a bruising landing if one should fall.

PHOTO BY JOE KENT

Otherwise, the variety of old cars, wagons, bicycles, motorcycles, and train cars are mildly interesting to preschoolers, but pretty fascinating to their dads and moms. The collection includes a car owned by Amelia Earhart with a seat that rolls out of its side like a drawer, venerable old Rolls Royces, a folding bicycle used by paratroopers, and a giant, steam-driven tractor. One of the most touching pieces is a small, white, ornate, horse-drawn hearse made to carry the caskets of babies. One of the most fun is an old tandem bicycle made for four riders—a great opportunity to relive *Bears on Wheels* by Stan and Jan Berenstain.

By the time we were finished with our visit, my preschooler was saying he was sick of old cars, but afterwards he kept talking about the things we had seen there. The Forney Museum was a fine diversion on a cold, sloppy spring day.

WHEN YOU GO:
Forney Museum

Phone Number: 303/ 297-1113

Website: www.forneymuseum.com

Address: 4303 Brighton Boulevard, Denver

Directions: From I-25, go east on I-70 to the Brighton Boulevard exit. Go right (southwest) on Brighton Boulevard just past 44th Street and look for the sign and museum entrance on the right.

Season: Year-round

Hours: Open to the public Monday through Saturday, 9 A.M. to 5 P.M.

Cost: $6.00 for adults; $4.00 for youth, ages 12–8; $3.00 for kids 6–11. Kids under 6 are free. Your ticket serves as a coupon for $1.00 off on your next visit. Discounts are available for groups.

Facilities: Large, unisex, wheelchair-accessible bathrooms are available with diaper decks. We found the toilet facilities *very* clean! There is a concession area with plastic tables and chairs and a pop machine for you to bring your own lunch. The museum is wheelchair and stroller accessible, and it has a gift shop with mostly train and car memorabilia.

Preschoolers' Comments: "I will buy this train to drive away when I grow up to be an engineer!"

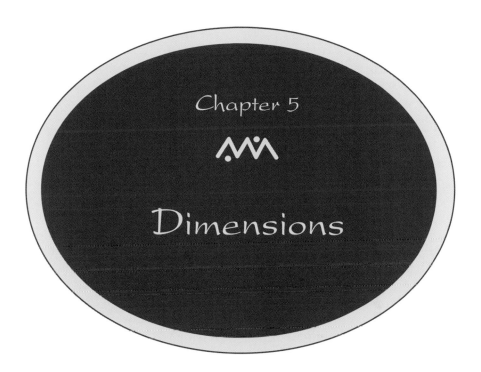

Chapter 5

Dimensions

CONNECTING TO THEIR PLACE IN THE WORLD

MOST YOUNG CHILDREN LOVE TO PLAY with concepts of dimension (though they may not realize it). Kids are forever imagining what it would feel like to be a giant or to be tiny. We've listed three Denver area attractions here that provide an opportunity to experiment with dimension and are appropriate for the youngest age groups. All are guaranteed to tickle your youngster's fancy!

PHOTO BY JOE KENT

Enrichment Ideas:

1. Break out the dolls! Dollhouses and dolls are perfect for introducing kids to the skill of viewing the world from others' perspectives. Get down on the floor and make your dolls talk. Encourage your kids to make their dolls talk back and then follow your child's lead. It is a fantastic window into your kid's mind as she or he takes you to places you would never have imagined.

2. Two classics stand out in children's literature on the subject of disproportionate size. Helen Palmer first wrote *A Fish Out of Water* in 1961, and *Clifford, the Big Red Dog* by Norman Bridwell was copyrighted in 1984. Still in print, these books are as much fun today as when they were first created. Looking at dimensions from the other direction is *The Little Red Ant and the Great Big Crumb*, a Mexican fable told by Shirley Climo. It carries a message of self-reliance while viewing the world from very close to the ground.

PHOTO BY JOE KENT

Tiny Town

Is your preschooler sick of being small? Hidden in the pine-covered hills just west of Denver is a little place guaranteed to give your tot a big lift.

Tiny Town *is* diminutive. It's a place where 2-year-olds can crouch down to peer through post-office windows and risk bumping their heads on the firehouse doors. A church can boast of a standing-room-only crowd when 6 toddler buddies celebrate inside by laughing and jumping up and down.

Begun in 1915, Tiny Town was originally on the Denver-to-Leadville stagecoach line. A Denver businessman started it by erecting buildings on a 1/6 scale to delight his young daughter. A series of floods and a fire later brought Tiny Town to ruin, and in 1987 any buildings that remained were put on the auction block.

Coloradoans responded by volunteering to fix the old buildings and make new ones. A not-for-profit foundation was formed, and through its efforts, the site has been completely renovated. Any excess revenues are now donated to local charities.

Photo by Susan Maly

Today, meticulously swept paths meander past gingerbread houses and miniature schools. Adults will appreciate the careful research and craftsmanship in the replicas of famous Colorado landmarks. Many buildings house doll-sized furnishings and implements.

Tiny Town's biggest hit is the train pulled by a peewee steam-driven locomotive. The train's small scale makes it a bit of a crunch for big folks but perfect for kids. Coal smoke wafts around the depot, and the unmistakable hoot of a steam whistle echoes

Photos by Joe Kent

down the canyon when the train crosses its small trestle. The clanging brass bell fits the turn-of-the-century scene perfectly.

Tiny Town has a shady picnic area and a playground in addition to its dwarf buildings and streets. The snack bar offers a limited menu but is dressed up with hanging flower baskets and big-band music playing in the background. Its gift shop has an array of souvenirs and train toys to help the shortest members of the family remember their lofty day. Toddlers' parents will appreciate the spotless men's and women's restrooms, both sporting diaper decks.

WHEN YOU GO:
Tiny Town

Phone Number: 303/ 697-6829

Address: 6249 South Turkey Creek Road, Tiny Town

Directions: From I-25, take U.S. Route 285 (Hampden Avenue) west into the mountains. Five miles past the C-470 junction, turn left onto South Turkey Creek Road. Drive through the canyon ½ mile and look for Tiny Town on the north side of the road.

Season: Weekends only in May, September, and October. Daily, Memorial Day through Labor Day.

Hours: 10 A.M. to 5 P.M.

Cost: Admission is $3.00 for adults, $2.00 for kids 3–12 years old, and free for anyone under 3. Train rides are $1.00 per ride, no matter how old you are. Parking is free.

PHOTO BY SUSAN MALY

Colorado Midland Railway

∧∧∧

A STREAM OF KIDS AND PARENTS FLOWED down steep stairs and into the stone-walled underbelly of Denver's Union Station. In the middle of a dark hallway (which seems more like a tunnel), light and a hum of activity spilled from a doorway.

Inside, youngsters, many on their dads' shoulders, lined a blue plywood half-wall. In front of them sprawled mountain ranges and rivers, mining claims and railroad trestles—a huge diorama of tiny proportion.

At the Colorado Midland Railway, locomotives the size of large toothpaste boxes snake along miniature rail lines, and long tails of boxcars and flatbeds slither behind. Pebbles become boulders in pretend streams made of glue, and dried, painted herbs look like towering aspen trees.

∧∧∧

At the Colorado Midland Railway, locomotives the size of large toothpaste boxes snake along miniature rail lines, and long tails of boxcars and flatbeds slither behind.

∧∧∧

Since 1937, the Denver Society of Model Railroaders has been envisioning and crafting a Colorado tour for its fleet of O-scale model trains. Their collective work has resulted in the largest O-scale railway layout in the world, with more than 6,000 square feet in the operating area.

The display is so large that when the trains run, dispatchers sit at elevated control panels, their heads nearly touching the ceiling, in order to see the tracks across the room. They communicate with sentries wearing T-shirts and radio headsets who pace cleverly hidden access routes. These workers dive under mountains and reemerge in canyons to reset derailed cars and flick debris from the rails with a pinky finger.

Often many trains run at once, and although there is not much for preschoolers to interact with here, just checking out the miniature details is pretty entertaining. (In one spot, a teensy bear is raiding white, boxy beehives while a little plastic man dances and waves from a nearby hill.)

Often many trains run at once, and although there is not much for preschoolers to interact with, just checking out the miniature details is pretty entertaining.

The biggest drawback is that kids need to be lifted up to see much of the display. A backpack carrier comes in very handy here. Also, the viewing area becomes congested during the evening's peak.

Nonetheless, when visited after a stroll through the cavernous Union Station waiting room, the Colorado Midland Railway is a terrific way to play with size and scope.

WHEN YOU GO:
Colorado Midland Railway

Phone Number: Colorado Midland Railway: 303/ 572-1015; Union Station: 303/ 534-6336

Address: 1701 Wynkoop Street, Denver

Directions: Union Station is in lower downtown Denver, on Wynkoop Street between 16th Street and 18th Street. Its massive front entrance gazes up the length of 17th Street. One of the easiest ways to get there is to ride the Light Rail "C" Line right down to Union Station.

The model railroad display is inside. Look for the gift shop at the west end of the waiting room. Across from the gift shop is a narrow hallway leading downstairs. Follow the signs to the Colorado Midland Railway.

Season: September through May

Hours: The model train area is open to the public the last Friday of each month from 7 P.M. to 9 P.M. Open Christmas night, 7 P.M. to 9 P.M., and the Saturday of the Parade of Lights, 2 P.M. to 4 P.M. Call ahead to confirm special holiday times.

Cost: Free, but donations are appreciated

Facilities: An elevator allows strollers and wheelchairs to descend into the basement of Union Station; however, the train viewing area is cramped and tall boards obstruct the view for those sitting at a low level. Kids need to be lifted up to see. There are bathrooms on the main level of Union Station with diaper decks. An old-fashioned lunch counter on the main level is also open when Amtrak is due in.

Special Considerations and Notes: The operators are serious about creating a family destination here. They insist that no smoking, cussing, or alcohol are allowed.

Preschoolers' comments: "We can't ride on these trains—we're too big!"

∧∧∧

When visited after a stroll through the cavernous Union Station waiting room, the Colorado Midland Railway is a terrific way to play with size and scope.

∧∧∧

Cherry Creek Mall Playground (Kid's Kourt)

∧⋎∧

LAUGHING AND SLIDING, a pair of 3-year-olds staggered and tried to stay balanced as they attempted to stand together, in their sock feet, on top of a giant egg yolk. That feat accomplished, they raced for a ripple of bacon, which became an easy-chair for lounging.

Meanwhile, other kids hopped into bowls of milky shredded wheat, danced over waffle ridges with butter and syrup, or wrapped their arms around giant strawberries. The big breakfast playground at Cherry Creek Mall offers more than great activity for kids' bodies. It's also wonderful exercise for their brains as they experiment with the possibilities of proportions. And it's the one place where kids are welcome to play in their food.

The playground equipment is made of spongy plastic material, as is the floor of the play area. Planters with bench seats for parents and caregivers surround the entire space. Small tables and chairs are clustered nearby as well.

PHOTO BY JOE KENT

Visitors to the play area are asked to remove their shoes, and a sign reminds parents not to leave children unattended. However, things can still get kind of wild. Big kids sometimes run through the area and throw themselves on the spongy food, coming awfully close to toddlers sharing the space. Close supervision is a must, not only of your own child, but of the other kids as well. The environment is one of free-form fun, but it seems to work better when parents are out on the floor playing with their kids.

Especially popular (read: crowded) when the weather is nasty, the big breakfast playground will stick in a preschooler's memory. It spawns all kinds of imaginative play and is certain to be something they ask to visit over and over again.

WHEN YOU GO:
Cherry Creek Mall Playground (Kid's Kourt)

Phone Number: 303/ 388-3900

Website: www.shopcherrycreek.com

Address: 3000 East 1st Avenue, Denver

Directions: From I-25, take Speer Boulevard southeast until it turns into 1st Avenue. Or from the south, take I-25 to the University Boulevard exit and go north on University to 1st Avenue. The shopping center is on the southeast corner of University Boulevard and 1st Avenue. The playground is inside the mall at the east end of the lower level near Foley's.

Season: Year-round

Hours: The mall is open Monday though Friday, 10 A.M. to 9 P.M; Saturday, 10 A.M. to 7:30 P.M.; and Sunday, 11 A.M. to 6 P.M. Holiday hours vary.

Cost: Free

Facilities: Just up the mall from the Kid's Kourt is a well-thought-out diaper-changing area with a convenient hand sink. It is available for parents of either gender to use. The mall itself is stroller and wheelchair accessible; however, strollers are not allowed in the playground area. Several convenient food-court-type restaurants are close to the playground.

Chapter 6

Out in the
Open

NATURE'S LESSONS

It's been said that kids should have the inalienable right to mess around in the woods. Even babies can learn from hanging out outdoors. And the rewards of open-air adventures can be reaped years after the outing is over.

Time spent with nature will help teach youngsters to be aware of the world at large and their relationship to it. They can learn body awareness and how to care for themselves, whether it means putting on a jacket or finding out which trails are too steep to climb. Kids might also learn about other creatures and how they manage to live in a world without grocery stores and central heat.

Nature's patterns are repeated on tiny and huge scales, so that when a child diverts a stream's trickle he gets a lesson in hydrology and wave action and currents. If you go on no other field trips, take your kids out to the wilds!

Enrichment Ideas:

1. Pack a daypack with your little hiker. Include the following 10 essentials and talk about what each item is for and which ones are strictly for adults to use. Include:

- food and water (bring extra for emergencies);
- sun protection, including sunscreen, lip balm, sunglasses, and a hat;
- extra clothes and rain gear;
- a map and compass;
- a pocket knife;
- something to build a fire with like matches or a lighter;
- a flashlight;
- a first-aid kit;
- a whistle;
- a tarp or space blanket for rigging an emergency shelter.

2. Make a nature collage. Give your youngster a box or bag to collect items while hiking. Suggest they choose things that would be easy to glue on a piece of paper. Pinecones, grass, twigs, even sand can all make great collages. When you are back from the hike, pour glue in a plastic bowl and let the kids dip the collected items in the glue and then stick them to the paper. Dark paper, in shades of brown, dark green, or black, seem to work best. For sand, show them how to spread the glue on the paper with a spoon and then sprinkle the sand or dirt over it and pat it into place. When the collage is done, mat it on a slightly larger piece of brown cardboard. Then encourage your kids to talk about their collage, asking them questions about the materials and where they found them.

3. Here are some of our favorite books to read before and after visiting a nature center and hitting the trails: In Nancy Shaw's *Sheep Take a Hike* kids can see how a group of sheep pack for a hike, head out, get lost, stumble into a bog, and eventually find their way home; *Around the Pond: Who's Been Here?* by Lindsay Barrett George takes kids on a hunt for blueberries, but they find much more in the beautiful illustrations. Also check out the "Four Seasons" series by Maria Rius. Use the appropriate book (*Winter, Spring, Summer, Fall*) as a springboard for conversation about seasonal signs that you saw or will see on your nature hike.

Chatfield Nature Preserve

∧∧∧

THE ENTRANCE TO THE CHATFIELD NATURE PRESERVE is down a long drive between grassy meadows, then past antique farm equipment, low wooden barns and corrals, and rustling cottonwood trees. It felt like we were driving onto the set of a Robert Redford western film.

The Chatfield Nature Preserve, on the edge of the foothills southwest of Littleton, has 700 acres with prairie grasses, beaver ponds, flower gardens, a survival garden of plants used by Native Americans and early settlers, old farm buildings, and an 1870s one-room schoolhouse. Outside the schoolhouse, kids can play on seesaws and swings near picnic tables in the dappled shade. A sign nearby warns visitors to beware of rattlesnakes.

PHOTO BY JOE KENT

Preschoolers seem most interested in the buildings of Hildebrand Farm, first settled in the 1860s. The white clapboard house, with its many additions and white picket fence, is a prominent feature of the site. Behind it, a summer kitchen sits on the banks of Deer Creek and is connected to the main house by a covered walkway. Also close by is a historic two-hole outhouse—with one seat the perfect height for toddlers!

Chickens, ducks, and turkeys scratch in the yard, but they are penned up at night to keep them safe

from local coyotes. In a chicken coop, we saw several hens resting on their nests and watching visitors with bright eyes when the visitors peered in the window. Extroverted sheep and goats rubbed against the rails of their corral and seemed to enjoy the patting and scratching of little hands.

Unfortunately, when we visited, most of the buildings were locked up, and the brochures for the self-guided tour were all gone. As a historic site, the Chatfield Nature Preserve did not have much to offer, and the kids' interest was soon worn out.

However, in October, the Chatfield Nature Preserve hosts a Pumpkin Festival, and kids can come and pick their own pumpkins from the huge pumpkin patch planted just for that purpose. The Front Range Antique Power Association provides hayrides to and from the pumpkin patch on wagons pulled by old tractors. Also in the fall, kids can wind their way through a giant maze cut into a cornfield. A tower oversees the field to make sure no one gets lost for good.

In addition to the historic farming parts of the nature pre-

serve, the area offers opportunities for wildlife watching along trails through grasslands and wetlands, and along a woodland creek. Many bird species, raccoons, deer, elk, hawks, and beaver use the preserve. Just days before our arrival, one visitor reported seeing a hungry black bear!

If you call ahead, you may be able to arrange a tour, and they will tailor it for preschool-age kids. That may be just what is needed to make this a really good field trip for the 6-and-under crowd.

WHEN YOU GO:
Chatfield Nature Preserve

Phone Number: 303/ 973-3705

Website: www.botanicgardens.org/chatfld.htm

Address: 8500 Deer Creek Canyon Road, Littleton

Directions: From C-470, take Wadsworth Boulevard south less than ½ mile to Deer Creek Canyon Road. Turn west and look for the entrance road on the left.

Season: Open all year except Thanksgiving and Christmas Day

Hours: Open to the public 9 A.M. to 5 P.M.

Cost: Admission to the nature preserve is $5.00 per carload. The first Friday of each month is free.

Facilities: The bathroom building, located near the old schoolhouse, is wheelchair accessible but does not have diaper decks. Drinking-water fountains are located at the bathroom building. There is no place to buy food, but shaded picnic tables are provided. Most trails are wheelchair and stroller accessible.

Special Considerations and Notes: Pets, bicycles, and skates are prohibited.

Lookout Mountain Nature Center and Preserve

∿∿

A BROWN BEAR LICKS SWARMING ANTS FROM HIS PAWS and greets visitors as they step inside the Lookout Mountain Nature Center. Unfortunately, he was killed by a car but is now the stuffed centerpiece of beautiful, open dioramas of the ponderosa pine forests. Behind him, a fox trots off with a freshly killed mouse in its teeth. The settings also include trees, flowers, grasses, birds, a deer, and a mountain lion, in addition to the bear and the fox.

Because they are open and in the middle of the room, little (and big) hands can hardly resist touching the fragile displays. So the dioramas are surrounded with stuff to mess with—all built within a toddler's reach. You can stroke flicker feathers and bear and fox fur, and you can play with a huge raindrop. Or you can lift a log and see burrowing creatures, and check out a button and light board describing territory from prairie grass to tundra. One display allows visitors to feel real mountain lion paws. The fur is silky soft and the claws are almost razor sharp. Even if you are careful, they will poke you, so touch gently.

∿∿

You can stroke flicker feathers and bear and fox fur, and you can play with a huge raindrop. Or you can lift a log and see burrowing creatures and check out a button and light board describing territory from prairie grass to tundra.

∿∿

A nearby room has nature books and toys for the youngest visitors, including a stuffed caterpillar with removable cushy rings, and spongy butterfly and beetle puzzles. Meanwhile, the sound system plays a melody of local birdsongs.

Outside, the Lookout Mountain Preserve offers shaded picnic tables and 1.4 miles of easy, scenic trails. These are perfect for intro-

ducing preschoolers to hiking. The loops are short enough for little legs to make the trek, and the Meadow Trail offers a variety of scenery. It curves through ponderosa pine forests, grasslands, and aspen glades, providing views of the high peaks and the city and prairies to the east. Although strollers could navigate some of the trails, a backpack baby carrier makes more sense. Our toddlers did get tired on the climb back to the museum building and needed a ride.

The Lookout Mountain Nature Center and Preserve is a mellow outing perfect for broadening kids' understanding of the natural world.

Phone Number: 303/ 526-0594

Website: open www.co.jefferson.co.us; search for "Lookout Mountain Nature Center."

Address: 910 Colorow Road, Golden

Directions: From I-25, go west on I-70 to the Lookout Mountain exit (exit #256) and turn right. An immediate left puts you on U.S. 40 going west. Follow the brown highway signs to the nature center. Stone gates mark the entrance.

Season: Year-round

Hours: The nature center is open to the public Tuesday through Sunday from 10 A.M. to 4 P.M. The preserve is open from 8 A.M. until dusk.

Admission: Free

Facilities: Although both bathrooms are wheelchair accessible, only the women's room has a diaper deck. The nature center and parts of the trails are stroller and wheelchair accessible. Picnic tables are provided outside, but if it is raining, there isn't a good place to eat. The nature center also has a nice selection of gift items offered for specified donations.

Special Considerations and Notes: The popular Toddler Time is a half-hour program held on one Thursday and one Saturday morning a month. Start times are 10:30 and 11:15. You must sign up in advance to attend. Group programs are also offered for preschool groups.

PHOTO BY JOE KENT

Theo Carson Nature Center
and South Platte Park

ᗺ

"I WANT TO SEE HOW COLD THE WATER IS," my preschooler insisted for the third time. Twice already he had clambered over rocks and bushes to trail his chubby fingers in the South Platte River's late summer flow. This time as he straightened up, hands dripping, he saw a fascinating sight. "Look at that big spider web!" he remarked, as he watched the spoked filaments glint in the sun. Then he hunkered down to study the structure and the creature that had spun it.

Later, as his little feet lagged and his little head bent beneath the warm sun, we sought the shade of a cottonwood tree for a water break. When we stepped from the path, a shy garter snake wove away from us through the grass, happy to let us have his spot beneath the tree. To a musical background of droning bees and clicking grasshoppers, we munched our snacks and soaked in

PHOTO BY JOE KENT

the fresh air. It smelled like baked grass and cotton-wood bark and moist river-banks. A bicycling family waved from the bike path a few yards away. What a wonderful antidote to the hustle of our busy lives!

The South Platte Park is a 648-acre oasis in the midst of the sprawling Denver metro area. Stretching north along the South Platte River from C-470, 35 percent of it is cov-ered by water, creating a wide variety of "neighbor-hoods" for resident wildlife. During the spring migra-tion, it is possible to see as many as 50 species of birds in one day. The area is home to fox, beaver, muskrat, skunk, raccoon, coyote, frogs, toads, lizards, and turtles. And it is the site of the Theo L. Carson Nature Center.

In 1992, this nature center was dedicated and opened to the public. Housed in the original home of early Littleton pioneers, it offers young children a wealth of activities to help them appreci-ate and understand the wildlife of the South Platte Park. Not only are there the typical stuffed animals and still dioramas that one often finds in nature centers, but at Theo Carson, kids can actu-ally hold a bull snake or a box turtle. And there is a skin table with pelts of different animals, allowing children to compare the texture of different kinds of fur.

But what this nature center is best at is helping preschoolers connect what they see inside with the actual plants, animals,

and landforms outside. Adults can check out explorer packs for the little ones to use when tromping around, and the staff has great advice on what to see and where to go with the kids. One flyer, entitled "58 Ways to Introduce Your Child to Nature," is perfect for preschool-age explorers and is a great tool for their parents and teachers.

Open year-round, the Theo Carson Nature Center and South Platte Park are terrific, nearby getaways in any season.

When You Go:
Theo Carson Nature Center and South Platte Park

Phone Number: 303/ 730-1022
Website: www.ssprd.org
Address: 7301 South Platte River Parkway, Littleton
Directions: From I-25, take South Santa Fe Drive south to Mineral Avenue. Turn right (west) on Mineral and right again on Platte River Parkway, just past the RTD Park-n-Ride. Follow the Platte River Parkway around the curve to the west and into

the parking lot for the Theo Carson Nature Center. Check the website for a map.

Season: Year-round; closed on major holidays

Hours: Park hours are sunrise to sunset. The nature center is open Tuesday through Friday, noon to 4:30 P.M.; Saturday and Sunday, 9:30 A.M. to 4:30 P.M.

Cost: Free. The Theo Carson Nature Center does offer a "Babes in the Woods" program twice during the summer for ages 3 and under, which costs $5.00. And 4-to-6-year-olds can attend Kid Nature Explorers on 4 consecutive Mondays from 9:30 A.M. to 11:30 A.M. for $42.00

Facilities: The nature center has bathrooms (with no diaper decks) and a drinking fountain. It is stroller and wheelchair accessible, but you are requested to leave strollers outdoors. There is a deck with benches for picnics. The park has 2½ miles of cement trail, and some natural-surface trails are accessible to strollers, weather and ground conditions permitting.

Special Considerations and Notes: The cement bike trail is popular with in-line skaters and cyclists, many of whom zip along at quite a clip. Staff of the nature center suggest getting little kids onto the dirt trails that wind through the grasses as soon as possible to avoid accidents.

〜
When we stepped from the path, a shy garter snake wove away from us through the grass, happy to let us have his spot beneath the tree. To a musical background of droning bees and clicking grasshoppers, we munched our snacks and soaked in the fresh air. It smelled like baked grass and cottonwood bark and moist riverbanks. A bicycling family waved from the bike path a few yards away. What a wonderful antidote to the hustle of our busy lives!
〜

Chapter 7

Old West

THEIR PLACE IN HISTORY

ONE OF THE BEST THINGS ABOUT THE DENVER AREA is its colorful history. From the different Native American tribes that lived in or frequented this area through the gold rush and mining days, and the farming and cowboy days, to the Front Range megalopolis that it is today, there's never been a boring moment in its entire history. Even better, the Denver area is rich in historic sites and history museums.

Especially fun are living-history museums, where the staff and volunteers dress in period costumes and reenact life as it was in the past. There is hardly a better way for young kids to get a taste of how things were in the olden days. These sites are terrific at helping children make the connection that historic people were a lot like us, and that the things they did and the decisions they made still affect us today. With that awareness, young lads and lasses can build a good foundation for understanding their own place in history.

Enrichment Ideas:

1. Play dress up. Go to the thrift store (or to your basement) and find old clothes that the kids can put on to play different characters in history. Broad roles work best; for example, a school marm, a cowboy, a farmer, a miner, a shopkeeper, or a boardinghouse proprietor. As the kids play, remind them that in the olden days they didn't have electric lights, cars, refrigerators, TV, computers, and so on. Ask them what they would do if they didn't have those things to work or play with.

2. Develop your own family's oral history. Tell your little ones a true story about when you were a child, or when grandpa or grandma was a child. Connect your story to the experience of your child, yet talk about how things were different as well. Nothing gives children a better sense of the continuity and the changes through time than when the people they know are the characters of the stories.

3. Read *A Little Prairie House, A Farmer Boy Birthday*, and others in the series of picture books based on the classics by Laura Ingalls Wilder. With beautiful illustrations inspired by Garth Williams, this series offers pre-readers a look at pioneer life and a foretaste of the great children's literature awaiting them in their elementary school years.

PHOTO BY JOE KENT

Littleton Historical Museum

∧∧∧

"CLANK-TINK, CLANK-TINK" SOUNDS from the blacksmith shop floated over chickens pecking their way through the barnyard. Inside,
a smudged and burly man poked iron rods into hot coals. When
they glowed neon orange, he pounded them into beautiful, twist-
ed shapes. Then, with a giant hiss, a cloud of steam, and a clunk
on the table, he finished the piece—a cast-iron kettle holder.

The Littleton Historical Museum's guides and docents, dressed
in buckskin and calico, turned what was potentially a ho-hum
tour of a historic site into an engaging visit for our toddlers.

PHOTO BY JOE KENT

Whether it was a woman
spinning yarn, a man feeding
the horses, or a farm wife stir-
ring potato soup over the
wood-burning stove, the museum people were friendly and
open and described their work
so that our preschoolers could
understand. This was the way
things were done in Littleton
a hundred years or more ago.

While gold was being dug
from the mountains to the
west, farmers were drawn to
the South Platte River's rich
bottomland. They supplied
food to the miners and a good
living to their families. The
Littleton Historical Museum
told our little ones their story.

The museum building
itself has exhibits of memorabilia from Littleton's early
days, while outside are two

farms. One is a replica of an 1860s homestead, while the other depicts life at the turn of the nineteenth century. Both have gardens, period equipment, and farm animals. The homestead's livestock reflects the great degree of self-sufficiency needed by a family during those times. The oxen are impressively huge, and our kids loved scratching and grunting at the pigs. However, they had the most fun discovering hens on their nests, hidden in the hay in the turn-of-the-century barn.

Situated on the edge of Ketring Lake, next to Ketring Park, the Littleton Historical Museum is a beautiful, peaceful setting that makes it a favorite with the preschool set.

PHOTO BY JOE KENT

Phone Number: 303/ 795-3950

Website: www.littletongov.org/museum

Address: 6028 South Gallup Street, Littleton

Directions: From I-25, take Broadway south to Littleton Boulevard. Turn right (west) on Littleton Boulevard and go about ¾ mile to Gallup Street. Turn left on Gallup and travel just under ½ mile to the museum entrance on the east side of the street. Check the website for a map.

Season: Year-round; closed on major holidays

Hours: Tuesday through Friday, 8 A.M. to 5 P.M.; Saturday, 10 A.M. to 5 P.M.; Sunday, 1 P.M. to 5 P.M. Closed Mondays.

Admission: Free to the general public

Facilities: The museum building and most paths throughout the farm are stroller and wheelchair accessible, although strollers are not allowed in the historic buildings. Both men's and women's restrooms are in the main museum building and have diaper decks. No pets, smoking, or food are allowed on the museum grounds. However, the museum is situated within Ketring Park, which has picnic tables under huge shade trees.

ᶺᶺᶺ

Our kids had the most fun discovering hens on their nests,
hidden in the hay in the turn-of-the-century barn.
Situated on the edge of Ketring Lake, next to Ketring Park,
the Littleton Historical Museum is a beautiful, peaceful setting
that makes it a favorite with the preschool set.

ᶺᶺᶺ

Four Mile Historic Park

∿∿

LEAVING OUR CAR IN A DIRT PARKING LOT, we passed through a cottage-shaped welcome gate and wandered up a dusty track, approaching Four Mile House as travelers did 140 years ago—on foot. We stepped out of the way as a horse-drawn stagecoach rumbled past, and we smiled at a Native American man in buckskin leggings who looked up from his work beside his teepee and nodded at us. Beneath a huge shade tree, a woman in swaying hoopskirts settled herself behind a spinning wheel and began to wind loose wool fibers into thread.

Built around 1859 and serving as a stage stop until 1870, Four Mile House was a key component in early Denver history. The homestead was located on Cherry Creek and represents a convergence of Native American and pioneer cultures. Today it has the oldest standing building in Denver. It is also the site of the 12-acre Four Mile Historic Park, an island of rural yesteryear in the heart of a booming metropolis.

∿∿
Built around 1859 and serving as a stage stop until 1870, Four Mile House was a key component in early Denver history.
∿∿

Several times a year, the historic park hosts special events, during which volunteers dress in period costumes and demonstrate what life was like for folks heading to Denver and the goldfields beyond. Stagecoach and covered-wagon rides, ice cream, old-fashioned games, crafts, and folk music are often a part of the demonstration. When we visited on the 4th of July, both Uncle Sam and Abraham Lincoln put in appearances.

But preschoolers may get the best understanding of what pioneer life was like on hot summer afternoons when the place seems almost deserted. Cicadas buzz in the trees, and the golden-brown smell of baking prairie grass wafts around antique wagons, a

vegetable garden, and the root cellar. A hint of a breeze may ruffle the clothes hanging from a crude line, and sleepy horses swish their tails and stamp their feet to keep flies away.

The overwhelming feeling is one of quiet and steady work. No cars rush by, no radios chatter from a distance, and no air-conditioners whine in the background or wash over you with an artificial chill. The stillness and slower pace may be the most important lesson Four Mile Historic Park has to offer. For us, it was a long, cool drink of calm in a busy day.

WHEN YOU GO:
Four Mile Historic Park

Phone Number: 303/ 399-1859

Address: 715 South Forest Street, Glendale

Directions: From I-25, exit onto Colorado Boulevard and go north to Cherry Creek Drive South. Turn right (east) on Cherry Creek Drive South and take the first left (north) on Cherry Street. Cross Cherry Creek itself and turn immediately right (east) on Exposition Avenue. Look for the entrance on the right.

Season: Year-round

Hours: April through September, Wednesday through Friday, noon to 4 P.M.; weekends, 10 A.M. to 4 P.M. October through March, weekends only, noon to 4 P.M. Horse-drawn rides, weekends only, noon to 2 P.M.

Admission: Free to enter the historic park except during special events. Special events are $5.00 for adults, $3.00 for seniors and kids 6–15, and free for kids under 6. Tours are $3.50 for adults and $2.00 for seniors and kids 6–15.

Facilities: Strollers and wheelchairs can access almost the entire area; however, the Four Mile House itself is mostly inaccessible. Bathrooms are located in the entrance building, down the dirt track from the other buildings, and do not have diaper decks. The park offers several picnic tables beneath shade trees, but there are no food concessions. A small gift shop has a wonderful variety of pioneer toys and memorabilia.

Buffalo Bill's Grave
and Museum

∧∧∧

WINDING UP LOOKOUT MOUNTAIN ROAD on the way to Buffalo Bill's Museum and Grave, I was unprepared for the view that greeted us as we rolled into the parking lot. Denver and the vast plains stretched eastward while the snowcapped teeth of the Rockies reared to the west. I knew immediately why Buffalo Bill, an icon of the Old West, wanted to be buried here. Few places have such a sweeping panorama of peak and prairie from one spot.

A short walk through a fringe of ponderosa pines led us to Buffalo Bill's grave. The path climbed through wildflowers and lichen-covered rocks to an iron fence surrounding the gravesite. Chunky white-quartz-studded cement covered Buffalo Bill and his wife and sparkled in the sun. A current of air brushed the hilltop and lifted an American flag on a nearby pole. In spite of the groups of tourists lingering about and snapping photos, it was a peaceful spot.

PHOTO BY JOE KENT

Perched at 7,375 feet above sea level, the Buffalo Bill Museum and Grave is one of the most popular attractions in Colorado, with all the trappings of a tourist destination. The original museum building, the Pahaska Tepee (*sic*) is named after Buffalo Bill's Yellowstone hunting lodge. An old plaster Indian greets visitors when they enter, and the place is packed to the eaves with brightly colored place mats, ashtrays, cowboy toys, Colorado mugs, postcards, Indian jewelry, stuffed animals, tumbled rocks, fool's gold, and a surprisingly good collection of books on western lands and lore.

The kid-friendly snack bar features homemade chili with buffalo meat as well as buffalo burgers and chili-cheese nachos. For dessert, there are several different varieties of fudge or a float made with locally brewed Duffy's root beer. The Pahaska Tepee embodies the intensely commercial side of Buffalo Bill's spirit.

The museum, however, allows visitors to seriously explore the historic contributions of one of the West's greatest showmen and entrepreneurs. From 1882 until 1913, Buffalo Bill conducted a Wild West Show with hundreds of performers shooting, riding, roping, and reenacting wagon-train attacks. As the extravaganza traveled from city to city, advertising posters preceded it, and the museum is full of these detailed works of commercial art. It also houses cases of artifacts, from show costumes to the glass balls that were tossed up in the air for sharpshooters to fire at. The displays are interesting for adults but are housed behind glass and are therefore inaccessible to little hands.

A quick stroll past the displays may be all that preschoolers are up for until they enter the kid's corral. Here, little ones can dress up in miniature cowboy clothes, including hats, vests, chaps, holsters, and fringed gloves. A pretend horse stands in front of a painted backdrop so that parents can take pictures of their little buckaroos on the range. A rope hangs over the saddle horn, handy for catching a plaster calf running in front of the horse. There is even a display and directions on how to spin a lariat. Kids can practice with ropes cut the perfect length for a 3-year-old.

A quick stroll past the displays may be all that preschoolers are up for until they enter the kid's corral. Here, little ones can dress up in miniature cowboy clothes, including hats, vests, chaps, holsters, and fringed gloves.

Outside, the museum's observation deck has spotting scopes and picnic tables with a spectacular view. It is a perfect place to relax before the winding drive back down the mountain to Denver.

WHEN YOU GO:
Buffalo Bill's Grave and Museum

Phone Number: Museum, 303/ 526-0747; Pahaska Tepee, 303/ 526-9367

Website: www.buffalobill.org

Address: 987½ Lookout Mountain Road, Golden

Directions: From I-25, take I-70 west to the Buffalo Bill Grave exit (exit #256) and follow the signs to the museum. See the website for map.

Season: Year-round, weather permitting; closed Christmas Day.

Hours: May through October, all week, 9 A.M. to 5 P.M.; November through April, 9 A.M. to 4 P.M.; closed Mondays.

Admission: Adults $3.00; ages 6–15, $1.00; ages 6 and under are free.

Facilities: The museum and gravesite are stroller and wheelchair accessible, and the museum has bathrooms with diaper decks; however, the Pahaska Tepee is not so toddler friendly.

Special Considerations: The museum conducts a program for preschool groups called The Mighty Buffalo. Phone 303/ 526-0747 for information and reservations.

Chapter 8

Incredible
Edibles

YOU ARE WHAT YOU EAT

FOR PRESCHOOLERS WHO'VE GOT BUT A FEW YEARS under their belt, much of the world is just what it is. For example, at mealtimes, food just appears in front of them on the table. If they think about it at all, they know it got there because mom or dad cooked it. Often they don't follow the supply chain back any further than that.

That's why it is so much fun to take them to visit sites along that food chain from field to table. Most food manufacturers in Denver don't offer tours to the public, and when they do, young children are often not allowed. (One notable exception is the Coors Brewery in Golden, which offers tours to all ages. However, we were a bit squeamish about the appropriateness of a brewery tour for preschoolers. If you are interested, call their information line at 303/ 277-BEER.) Nevertheless, there are a few places worth taking kids to see, introducing them to the world of food production on the grand scale.

Enrichment Ideas

1. Make your own homemade butter. Pick up some whipping cream from the dairy case at the grocery store. Pour the cream in a deep bowl. (If you want yellow butter, color the cream by grating a carrot into it. After a few minutes, strain the carrot out by pouring the cream through a sieve or strainer.) Beat the cream with an electric mixer until the fat starts to separate from the liquid (about 20 minutes). Keep beating until you have big lumps of fat. Pour the liquid into a bowl and pack the fat together into a mushy ball. Squeeze the excess liquid from this ball with a spatula. Now you have homemade butter to spread on toast. Also, the finished product will be unsalted. Try adding some salt to some of the butter. Which kind do your kids prefer?

2. Bake bread from scratch. Several yummy recipes can be found in the back of *Everybody Bakes Bread* by Norah Dooley. It is easier than you would imagine.

3. Before visiting farm, flour mill, or bakery, read *The Little Red Hen* and the *Ear of Wheat* by Mary Finch. It traces the steps from planting a grain of wheat to freshly baked bread while kneading in a moral of cooperation. Its colorful illustrations are great for toddlers. *The Milk Makers* by Gail Gibbons has clear descriptions and simple pictures, making this an excellent nonfiction book for youngsters. *Everybody Bakes Bread* by Norah Dooley introduces readers to different kinds of breads from around the world. It is a bit long for most preschoolers but can be abbreviated for younger kids.

PHOTO BY DIANE CLAUDE

Great Harvest Bread Company

〜〜

WITH A GRUNT, A BAKER AT THE GREAT HARVEST BREAD COMPANY lifted an armful of gooey dough onto the table. It landed with a heavy splat. Smells of yeast, warm flour, and a hint of cinnamon wafted around our noses as we watched him work.

"Would you like to come back and slap the dough?" the baker asked with a grin. My little boy wasn't sure. So the man cut off a little ball of dough and handed it to my son, who looked up at me, wondering what to do with it.

"Why don't you squish it?" I suggested. With a big smile, he did just that.

While he played with the dough, we watched the bakers at the Great Harvest Bread Company kneading loaf after loaf by hand. They dropped them into oiled loaf pans to let them rise again. Next, a man loaded trays with pans of risen bread

〜〜

With a grunt, a baker at the Great Harvest Bread Company lifted an armful of gooey dough onto the table. It landed with a heavy splat. Smells of yeast, warm flour, and a hint of cinnamon wafted around our noses as we watched him work.

〜〜

into a giant rotary oven, setting the dial to ensure they would emerge golden brown and perfectly done.

The bakers talked about the ingredients of the bread and the different varieties they bake. Later, after providing a wet paper towel for cleaning up dough-sticky hands, a baker sliced us each a piece of fresh-baked bread to sample.

Proud of their handmade breads, the owners and bakers of the Great Harvest Bread Company are happy to show off their works. You can stop in or call ahead to arrange a tour. The space is cramped, so strollers aren't a good idea. A backpack carrier for babies and toddlers will help keep them contained, safe, and out of the dough, while offering them a view of the process.

We brought home a loaf of bread and some cinnamon rolls to remind us of our visit, and to inspire conversation about how commercial bakeries can make so many loaves of bread at one time.

WHEN YOU GO:
Great Harvest Bread Company

Phone Number: 303/ 347-8767

Website: www.greatharvest.com

Address: 5910 South University Boulevard, Littleton

Directions: From I-25, take the Belleview Avenue exit (exit#199) and go west on Belleview Avenue. At University Boulevard, turn left (south) and go about 1 mile to Orchard Road. The Great Harvest Bakery is in the shopping center on the southeast corner of University and Orchard. Check the website for a map.

Season: Year-round

Hours: Store hours are 7 A.M. to 6 P.M. every day except Sunday. The best time to visit is 9:30 A.M. Tours are offered to groups of 15 or more on Tuesday and Thursday mornings. Make reservations 2 weeks in advance.

Cost: Free

Facilities: The front of the store is wheelchair accessible. Restrooms are not available.

Preschoolers' Comments: "Why did he ask me to slap the dough?"

ᴧᴧ

The bakers talked about the ingredients of the bread and the different varieties they bake. Later, after providing a wet paper towel for cleaning up dough-sticky hands, a baker sliced us each a piece of fresh-baked bread to sample.

ᴧᴧ

Arvada Flour Mills

THE FIRST THING YOU NOTICE ABOUT THE ARVADA FLOUR MILLS is its shiny silver color. The entire building is covered with a tin-and-steel alloy pressed in the shape of blocks. Preschoolers love running their hands over the surface and laughing at the silly bricks. Inside, the mill is shadowy and rustic, with unfinished raw-beam construction and rusty old machines still lurking throughout. The history of the place is so rich you can almost taste it.

PHOTO BY JOE KENT

At first we wondered if this field trip was appropriate for preschoolers. Our tour was detailed and disorganized and hard to follow. The mill isn't operating and has no moving parts to watch. Although the kids were allowed to feel the wheat and belts and grain buckets, our guide took no notice of their desire to do so.

Early on he lost our preschoolers' attention and we had to interpret the displays to our little ones. Eventually, our toddlers melted down and we had to walk away.

Still, this is a unique opportunity for kids to be exposed to a really different environment—the inside of an old food factory. Our kids learned that flour starts as stalks of wheat and that the seeds are called wheat berries. They saw a huge scale outside that once weighed farmers' wagons and the chute where those wagons dumped their loads of grain. They got lots of exercise climbing steps to the four different levels of the mill and discovering a wide variety of old machines that performed various functions, from washing the berries to sewing the flour sacks shut. They relished spinning the bins once used to wash the wheat berries and feeling the silk used to screen the water.

It is true that the preschoolers struggled to endure our guide, who focused more on the mill than on the needs of the children. However, the place itself provided an unparalleled opportunity to enrich their experience, to build their vocabulary, and to exercise their imaginations.

PHOTO BY JOE KENT

Photo by Joe Kent

If you plan ahead, this can be a fine trip for your little ones. First, when you call to make reservations, be sure they understand that you will be bringing preschoolers with short attention spans. Ask for a mini-tour—about 25 minutes at the longest. Next, bring at least one adult for every two kids; smaller groups are better, since some spaces inside the mill can be a tight fit. Third, make a rule that preschoolers must hold an adult's hand at all times when inside the mill building. Fourth, ask the guide to hit only the major highlights, keeping the explanations simple. Finally, ask if the kids can touch the wheat stalks, the old grain buckets, and the huge grinding wheels. It will make the tour far more meaningful for them.

ᨆ

Our kids learned that flour starts as stalks of wheat and that the seeds are called wheat berries. They saw a huge scale outside that once weighed farmers' wagons and the chute where those wagons dumped their loads of grain. They got lots of exercise climbing steps to the four different levels of the mill and discovering a wide variety of old machines that performed various functions, from washing the berries to sewing the flour sacks shut.

ᨆ

Phone Number: 303/ 431-1261

Address: 5590 Wadsworth Boulevard, Arvada

Directions: From I-25, take I-70 west to the Wadsworth Boulevard exit (exit #269B). Go north on Wadsworth just past 56th Avenue to Grandview Avenue. Turn left (west) on Grandview and travel through 4 blocks of Old Town Arvada to Olde Wadsworth Boulevard. Turn left and look for the flour mill just across the railroad tracks.

Season: Year-round

Hours: Tours by appointment only

Cost: $1.00 donation for adults and 50 cents for kids

Facilities: The mill building and tour are not stroller or wheel-chair accessible. Bathrooms are available, although they do not have diaper decks. There is an area that used to be a gift shop, and you can still buy a few booklets about the history of Arvada.

Special Considerations and Notes: The building is neither heated nor air-conditioned. It can be very cold inside during the winter and quite hot in the summertime. The best time to visit is in the fall or spring, when temperatures are moderate.

Preschoolers' Comments: (When looking up an old flour chute) "I like the pipes! When we look up them, all the wheat berries don't come pouring down on our heads!"

White Fence Farm

ᐰᐰ

OUTSIDE THE OK CORRAL AT WHITE FENCE FARM is a little vending machine. For a quarter, you get a handful of feed pellets for the animals in the corral. That little machine must be one of the biggest moneymakers at this establishment.

As parents plugged in their 25-cent pieces, little kids lined the split-rail fence and giggled and winced as gentle goats and a burro nibbled from outstretched hands. When they were done feeding the animals, the children lined up to wash their hands at a nearby pump.

White Fence Farm is as much an Americana theme park as it is a restaurant. Built on what was originally the Wilson family's 80-acre hay and cattle farm, it now has bridges over a babbling brook, a tree house and playground, an aviary full of peacocks, a carriage museum, and three different gift shops, in addition to the OK Corral. Kids can be kept pretty busy while waiting for a table.

ᐰᐰ

White Fence Farm has bridges over a babbling brook, a tree house and playground, an aviary full of peacocks, a carriage museum, and three different gift shops, in addition to the OK Corral.

ᐰᐰ

Meals here are served family style from dishes set in the middle of the table by the wait staff. Fried chicken is the most popular entrée, and side dishes include bean salad laced heavily with mayonnaise, coleslaw, and corn fritters. It turned out to be very basic Americana-style home cooking—a bit of a disappointment for this preschoolers' mom, who is actually kind of tired of home cooking. However, the portions are plentiful and the servers are exceptionally cheery and squeaky clean. Still, we found the prices a bit steep for the quality of the food.

But it is worth the price for the entertainment the kids can get out of the place. Whether it was poking their heads through holes in a painted animal board for pictures, or riding a horse-drawn carriage around the grounds, they had a ball. And they learned about commercial cooking on the kitchen expedition. The staff is happy to take visitors through many of the food-prep areas upon request.

This family-owned restaurant was designed and built to appeal to families. And it succeeds mightily.

WHEN YOU GO:
White Fence Farm

Phone Number: 303/ 935-5945

Website: www.whitefencefarm.com

Address: 6263 West Jewell Avenue, Lakewood

Directions: From I-25, take the 6th Avenue Freeway west to Sheridan Boulevard. Go south (left) on Sheridan about 3 miles to Jewell Avenue. Turn west (right) on Jewell and look for the White Fence Farm on the north side of the road.

Season: All year, except for the month of January, when they are closed for maintenance and staff vacations. Closed Thanksgiving Day and Christmas Day.

Hours: Tuesday through Saturday, 4:30 P.M. to 8:30 P.M.; Sunday, 11:30 A.M. to 8 P.M. Closed Mondays.

Cost: Entrees average $12.65, and kids' meals are about $7.00. Carriage rides are $3.00 per child and $4.00 for adults. A handful of feed pellets for the animals in the OK Corral is 25 cents.

Facilities: The restaurant and most of the grounds are stroller and wheelchair accessible, although some areas are too congested for easy maneuvering. Both men's and women's bathrooms have diaper decks, and additionally there are two "family restrooms," complete with stepstools, changing counters, and fun wallpaper. There are two gift shops full of knickknacks and toys, and in the Americana Barn you'll find Granny's Pie Shop, where you can buy pie, fudge, and drinks, and sit and listen to live music.

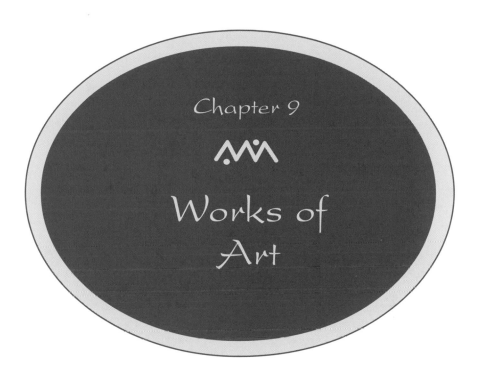

Chapter 9

Works of Art

It's a Natural

WHEN IT COMES TO ART, nothing seems to come more naturally to kids. Whether it is drawing with crayons on the linoleum or singing songs in the bathtub, preschoolers' wonderful lack of inhibition can lead them to express themselves in more ways than are imaginable. And, just as their own art often has a beautiful, wild reasoning to it, at some visceral level, kids can also appreciate and be fascinated by other's artwork, too. The early years are a perfect time to introduce art liberally, allowing kids to experience just a bit of what's possible in the realm of expression.

Enrichment Ideas:

1. Put on a show. Take advantage of the ham in your little one and stage a performance. Play a tape and have a free-form dance, or dress up and pretend you're in the theater, or get out the pot lids and wooden spoons and start up a band. The idea is not to do any of it well, but to experience the sheer joy of expressing yourself in front of an audience, even a pretend one.

2. Make art you can play on. Get a huge cardboard carton from an appliance store and remove all the staples, replacing them with tape. Next, decide if you want your playable art to stand up, lie down, or be mobile. Then cut out shapes (what suits your kids' fancy—straight-lined or curved?) to look through and perhaps to crawl through. Finally, decorate the box with paints, strips of colored cloth, crunched-up paper, glitter, leaves, and pinecones—you name it. Then name your sculpture, too! Does it look like something, or is it an abstract work? Have fun!

3. Read *Shape Space* by Cathryn Falwell. This wonderful, whimsical romp with a bunch of squares and semicircles takes on the rhythm of a dancer practicing her steps over and over again. Its darling pictures and the song of its text deserve countless repeat performances! *Katie and the Mona Lisa* by James Mayhew is a story that romps in and out of the frames of famous paintings. This engaging trip to an art museum introduces kids to the Mona Lisa (who says "*Mamma mia!*" a lot) and other giants of the Renaissance. *Little Mouse's Painting* by Maryjane Begin shows that art's appeal is often in seeing ourselves hidden within a work.

DENVER ART MUSEUM

Heritage Square Music Hall Children's Theater

∧∧∧

ROUND-EYED AND CURIOUS, Will, just over 3 years old, took Brer Rabbit's hand and clambered up onto the stage. There, he and three other preschoolers helped Brer Rabbit steal Brer Fox's peanuts from his garden.

The kids "picked" felt peanuts the size of large sippy cups and put them in Brer Rabbit's basket. Then they crawled under a fence and back to their seats in the audience. Once there, Will wiggled and giggled with his preschool buddies about his adventure on stage.

Heritage Square Music Hall's Children's Theater is ideal for even young preschoolers. During the week, the shows are often held midmorning and they last only an hour. As part of the show, actors come out into the hall and involve the audience in the per-

PHOTO BY JOE KENT

formance. The action moves along so that the kids can stay in their seats and be involved in the play the whole time. The unscripted parts, where the preschoolers are involved, keeps the cast on their toes, and the actors chuckle as they ad lib to the kids' off-the-wall contributions.

This is a great opportunity for kids to learn about theater in a relaxed setting that caters to their humor and short attention spans.

WHEN YOU GO:
Heritage Square Music Hall Children's Theater

Phone Number: 303/ 279-7800

Address: 18301 West Colfax Avenue, #D103, Golden

Directions: From Denver, go west on I-70 to the Morrison exit (exit #259). Go right on U.S. 40 just over a mile and look for the entrance to Heritage Square on the left. The Music Hall is on the Main Street of Heritage Square near the entrance on the right.

Season: Year-round

Hours: Saturday shows are at 1:30 P.M. and 3 P.M. Weekday performances are for school groups and day-care centers but are still open to the public on a space-available basis. Times vary, so call ahead. No meals are available with children's shows.

Cost: $5.00 for kids, $4.00 for adults over age 13. Target age: 2 to 12 years. Large school groups should book at least a month in advance to ensure space.

Facilities: The theater and bathrooms are wheelchair accessible, but strollers are a hassle here. Bathrooms do not have diaper decks. No food is available in the theater for the children's performances, and there is no gift shop.

Preschoolers' Comments: Cole (leaving the theater): "Did you like the music?" Amanda (dancing as she walks): "Did dee dum, did dee dee! Did dee dum, did dee dee!"

Swallow Hill
Summer Series

ᐱᐯᐱ

COTTONWOOD LEAVES RUSTLED as folks opened blankets and beach chairs on the lawn below. Fried chicken and pasta salad emerged from coolers, and hands waved to new arrivals. Soon, the strains of a banjo and guitar drifted over the crowd and before long, a full-scale bluegrass concert was underway. Within minutes, a gaggle of young children was bouncing and spinning to the music in front of the stage.

Every summer, Swallow Hill Music Association holds a series of folk-music concerts at the Four Mile Historic Park. Concerts last about an hour and fifteen minutes, and the casual atmosphere is perfect for families with energetic young ones.

PHOTO BY JOE KENT

The music is peppy and not too loud, and the audience is fairly tolerant of wigglers. If the kids get tired of listening to music or dancing, they can wander through the farm and look at animals. (Although this means the attendant parent will miss some of the concert.)

The concerts end at 8 P.M.—a good time for getting home and to bed.

WHEN YOU GO:
Swallow Hill Summer Series

Phone Number: 303/ 777-1003

Website: www.swallowhill.com

Address: Swallow Hill main office: 71 East Yale Avenue, Denver; Four Mile Historic Park: 715 South Forest Street, Glendale

Directions: Swallow Hill: From I-25, take Broadway south to Yale. The building is on the northeast corner of Yale and Broadway. The Shady Grove at the Four-Mile Historic Park: Take Colorado Boulevard to Cherry Creek Drive South (two blocks south of Alameda Avenue, in Glendale). Turn right (east) on Cherry Creek Drive South and take the first left (north) on Cherry Street. Cross Cherry Creek itself and turn right immediately onto Exposition. Look for the entrance to Four Mile Historic Park on the right. The Shady Grove is just east of the small house behind the visitor's center.

Season: June through August, except July 4th

Hours: Wednesdays, 6:30 P.M.

Cost: $4.00 for adults, $2.00 for kids 12 and under

Facilities: The dirt road and lawns within the Four-Mile Historic Park are stroller and wheelchair accessible, with some negotiation. Bathrooms are located at the entrance to the park and do not have diaper decks.

Denver Art Museum

∧∧∧

SNOOTY ART CONNOISSEURS SNIFFED AND GLARED as I bounced my fussy 1-year-old on my hip and scolded my 3-year-old: "Honey, take your tongue *off* that fifteenth-century oil painting!" This was a horrible fantasy of mine and the main reason why the Denver Art Museum was one of the last places we field-tested. Ten minutes into our visit, my mind changed like my mood does after a good night's sleep. The Denver Art Museum is now one of my favorite places to go with young kids.

Almost immediately, young visitors are swimming in art, not even knowing that they are laying a solid foundation for later appreciation and achievement. You enter the museum from a plaza between the art museum and the Denver Public Library. The cement paving stones are laid out in geometric patterns, and a huge sculpture invites kids to climb, slide, and bang on it.

DENVER ART MUSEUM/PHOTO BY LLOYD RULE

Inside, you can pick up the "Free Things for Kids to Do Today" booklet with a picture of Seymour, the monkey mascot. He appears at various locations throughout the museum to mark fun kids' activities.

Near the elevators, kids will encounter the Egyptian collar-making exhibit, where they use markers, tape, and string to make their own Egyptian neckware. They can plunge into an appreciation for the artists that made the real collars thousands of years ago. While the kids are working, parents and teachers can read interesting points from the reference books available and the exhibit itself.

Another option is to check out a family backpack. Available every day during the summer and on weekends during the school year, each backpack has a theme that corresponds to an exhibit within the museum. The most popular backpack is the jaguar, snakes, and birds backpack for the Mayan exhibit on the fourth floor. It is full of colorful items for children to manipulate, including a stuffed snake and cardboard templates to make a big bird-

beak mask. These tools, which encourage youngsters to use their hands, help instill a deeper understanding of the art displayed around them.

According to Lindsey Evans, family backpack coordinator at the museum, "Education is a focus here, and we encourage kids to pull things out of the backpack and have fun on the floor, right in the exhibit!"

The Denver Art Museum hints in other ways that preschoolers are very welcome. You'll find a stepstool tucked under the water fountain, a family restroom with a diaper deck and nursing area, free strollers for checking out (including strollers with infant carriers attached), and a kids menu with peanut-butter-and-jelly sandwiches at the Palettes snack bar.

But the most family-friendly space is the Just for Fun Center. Located on the C-level, it is full of hands-on activities to draw kids into the world of art. At a magnet board covered in beautiful pictures of the Pacific Northwest, children can manipulate photographs and native interpretations of local animals. They can put a picture of an eagle in the magnetic trees and an eagle totem right next to it, to appreciate how people artistically interpret their environment. Or they might play with a giant foam 3-D puzzle of a Mayan stone slab, or dress up in Egyptian animal costumes.

At the Denver Art Museum, there is always more to do than time will allow. Plan to visit often and explore one small section at a time. Art has never been less snooty or more fun.

WHEN YOU GO:
Denver Art Museum

Phone Number: 720/ 865-5000 (main number); 720/ 913-0049 (family and kids programs)

Website: www.denverartmuseum.org and www.wackykids.org

Address: 100 West 14th Avenue Parkway, Denver

Directions: From I-25, take the Colfax Avenue exit and go east on Colfax about 1½ miles to Bannock Street. Turn right (south) on Bannock and go one block to 14th Avenue. The Denver Art Museum is the tall silver building with lots of odd windows across from Civic Center Park.

Season: Year-round; closed on Independence Day

Hours: Closed Monday. Tuesday, open 10 A.M. to 5 P.M.; Wednesday, 10 A.M. to 9 P.M.; Thursday, Friday, and Saturday, 10 A.M. to 5 P.M.; Sunday, noon to 5 P.M.

Cost: $6.00 adults, kids 12 and under free. Saturdays, free to all Colorado residents.

Facilities: Stroller and wheelchair accessible, family bathroom with diaper deck, cafeteria, gift shop.

∧∨∧

But the most family-friendly space is the Just for Fun Center.
Located on the C-level, it is full of hands-on activities
to draw kids into the world of art.

∧∨∧

Arvada Center for the Arts and Humanities

∧∧∧

YOU SIT DOWN TO PRESERVE A PIECE OF YOUR COMMUNITY'S HISTORY, and the next thing you know, a sea serpent is hissing mist in your front yard. At the Arvada Center for the Arts and Humanities, you never quite know what will happen next.

The seeds of the Arvada Center sprouted when a schoolteacher wanted to preserve the oldest structure in Arvada in an effort to teach local history. The Haines log home became the centerpiece of the Arvada History Museum, and the Arvada Center for the Arts and Humanities grew around it. The original log house is still at the heart of this sprawling complex that hosts more than 300,000 visitors each year. And kids under six years old are some of the Arvada Center's most enthusiastic fans.

∧∧∧

You sit down to preserve a piece of your community's history, and the next thing you know, a sea serpent is hissing mist in your front yard. At the Arvada Center for the Arts and Humanities, you never quite know what will happen next.

∧∧∧

It is hard to know if they love the children's theater, the dress-up area in the history museum, or the outdoor art better. The children's-theater professionals perform three shows each season, for 60,000 youngsters. The youngest toddlers may not understand or follow the subject matter of some of the plays, so it is best to check ahead of time to decide whether or not to catch a currently running performance or to wait for a different show.

However, if the play is not the thing for your little one, the galleries and the history museum may be just the ticket. The Arvada Center emphasizes contemporary art with changing exhibits that often include touch/smell/see hands-on areas for kids and take-

home activity sheets. In the history museum, little ones can dress up as cowboys and pioneers and ride cute stuffed horses. Two participatory plays are offered in conjunction with museum tours if you book the tour ahead.

And when it is time to appreciate outdoor art, what could be better than a 343-foot-long, climbable sculpture named Squiggles? Surrounded by a sea of bright aquamarine rubber padding, this creation of local artist Bill Gian is covered by scales, each imprinted with its own little work of art. Part of the Arvada Center's playground, Squiggles was designed for 4- to 12-year-olds, but even babies can have fun patting and cruising along its colorful length. If the weather is hot, plan to play there at the top of the hour, when for five minutes or so, Squiggles hisses and sprays a cooling mist of water from its mouth, tail, and fins.

Finish up with a picnic on the grass near one of the other beautiful outdoor sculptures, and you've had a top-notch artistic preschool experience.

Phone Number: 303/ 431-3080 for general information and 303/ 431-3939 for the box office

Website: www.arvadacenter.org

Address: 6901 Wadsworth Boulevard, Arvada

Directions: From I-25, take I-70 west to the Wadsworth Boulevard exit (exit #269), and go north on Wadsworth about 2½ miles. Look for the entrance on the left (west) side of the street.

Season: Year-round

Hours: Gallery/museum open 9 A.M. to 5 P.M., Monday through Saturday, and 1 P.M. to 5 P.M. on Sunday. See their website or call for schedule of dates and show times.

Cost: Outdoor art, playground, galleries, and museum are free and open to the public. Call the box office for tour fees and performance prices.

Facilities: The playground and other facilities are wheelchair accessible. Both men's and women's bathrooms on the main floor have diaper decks, although the bathrooms closest to the playground do not. The Arvada Center sports a nice gift shop, but there is no snack bar or restaurant.

PHOTO BY DIANE CLAUDE

Chapter 10

Urban Parks

IF THERE EVER IS A PLACE NEAR TO A PRESCHOOLER'S HEART, IT IS A PARK. With endless green lawns, shade trees, and playgrounds, parks are the place for kids. Parks are out of the house and big enough to be an adventure, yet careful landscaping and amenities make them safer for little ones than, say, an abandoned lot. Little wonder that urban parks, especially ones with playgrounds, are Kidville, USA. Here are our favorites.

PHOTO BY JOE KENT

Enrichment Ideas:

1. Help your kids anticipate a visit to the park by reading one of the following books before you head out. *Park Beat – Rhymin' Through the Seasons* by Jonathon London combines bright, colorful illustrations with "rappin' and tappin' and finger-snappin'" verse to explore a year in the park. Other books like Alexandra Day's *Carl's Afternoon in the Par*k and Mathew Price's *In the Park* offer perspectives on differences between parks and playgrounds.

2. With your older preschoolers, make a map of the closest park. Use a big piece of green construction paper and draw bike paths, picnic tables, trees, and playground equipment on it. Don't forget details like trash cans and park benches. Now, make up stories about visitors to the park. Let your kids provide the names of the characters and key ideas about what those characters do. Allow the preschoolers to tell as much of the story as possible.

Belleview Park

∧∧∧

IT WAS TOO LATE TO TURN BACK. We had no choice but to go on. Soon the dark surrounded us, and we could see almost nothing. My son clutched my arm and my friend's daughter climbed into her lap. A few of the children around us screamed. Then it was over and the sun again warmed our heads as the train ride left the tunnel and chugged past shade trees and flowerbeds back to the station.

The next stop was a petting farm, with a fine selection of rabbits, goats, sheep, ducks, and a cow for the kids to meet. Small hoses overhead sprayed a cooling mist over people and beasts, and a convenient utility sink offered a good place to wash hands when the kids were done manhandling the animals.

After a picnic on the green lawns, a wade at the sandy ford of a meandering stream, and a swing through the playground, Belleview Park hit the top of our list of favorite summer outings.

PHOTO BY JOE KENT

Phone Number: 303/ 762-2680 or 303/ 798-6927

Website: www.ci.englewood.co.us, then click on "recreation" for information about the park

Address: 5001 S. Inca, Englewood

Directions: From I-25, go west on Belleview about 5 miles to Inca Drive. Turn right (north) on Inca and look for the parking lot on the left. Another parking lot is located on the west side of the park right off of Belleview.

Season: The park is open year-round, and the train and petting farm are open Memorial Day through Labor Day.

Hours: Park hours are sunrise to sunset. The train runs Tuesday through Saturday, 10 A.M. to 4 P.M., and on Sunday, 11 A.M. to 4 P.M. The petting farm is open Tuesday through Sunday, 10 A.M. to 4 P.M.

Cost: $1.00 per ticket for the train and the petting farm

Facilities: Bathrooms without diaper decks are available, as well as picnic tables and a playground.

Special Considerations and Notes: Bring extra water for washing grubby hands after visiting the animals. Also, a bathing suit and water shoes are nice if the kids want to play in the stream. If you are planning on bringing a day-care or preschool group, you must secure a permit at least 2 days ahead of your visit. The permit is free, but certain restrictions apply. Call 303/ 762-2680 for information.

PHOTO BY JOE KENT

Westlands Park

∧∧∧

THE ENTRANCE DRIVE TO WESTLANDS PARK passed beneath a sculpture shaped like an arch with cutouts of leaves, suns, moons, and hummingbirds. It was the first hint that this playground was something special.

We hiked up the sidewalk toward the voices of playing children and the ground dropped away before us. There, in a hollow between two hills, were swings, sandboxes, bridges, slides, playhouses, bouncy animals mounted on springs, and other things we'd never seen before.

The play areas are divided into three distinct spaces, each sized for and appealing to different age levels. The area with the most advanced equipment also had a concentration of older kids, and the peewee area sported more babies, but children are free to check out all three spaces. Our kids were most comfortable in the area meant for the youngest players, but they wanted to explore the whole playground by the end of our visit.

PHOTO BY JOE KENT

Against the west bank is a building with bathrooms, a drinking fountain, and picnic tables. Stairs climb the hill to sheltered picnic facilities overlooking the playground and extensive playing fields to the west.

Adjacent to the playgrounds, a dry creek is left in its natural state, with towering cottonwoods and lush underbrush. A bridge spans this area to a tall structure, reminiscent of a fire tower, complete with steep stairs to the highest lookout level.

Also near the playground, Westlands Park offers gardens, group picnic areas with barbecue

PHOTO BY JOE KENT

grills, wide sidewalks, and a huge sundial surrounded by benches and celestial etchings. There is a fountain sculpture of boulders, and the sidewalk slopes into its midst; you could roll a stroller right into the water. It instantly captivated our kids, despite a cool day and long pants and coats.

Lakes (one with a brass dolphin sculpture) and mountain views make Westlands Park a beautiful setting for an outing with the tots. No wonder it became incredibly popular (and often crowded) soon after it was built.

WHEN YOU GO:
Westlands Park

Phone Number: 303/ 773-0252 or 303/ 486-5773 for group permits

Website: www.greenwoodvillage.com and click on general information, then go to "parks, trails, and information"

Address: 5701 South Quebec Street, Greenwood Village

Directions: From I-25, take Orchard Road west to Quebec Street. Go north on Quebec Street about ¼ mile and look for the entrance on the west side of the street. Check the website for a map.

Season: Year-round

Hours: Park hours are sunrise to sunset

Cost: Free

Facilities: Both men's and women's bathrooms have diaper decks. The park is stroller and wheelchair accessible. There are no concessions nearby, so bring your own snacks or lunch.

Special Considerations and Notes: A sign near the fountain warns that the water is nonpotable; however, Greenwood Village treats and filters it before it comes out of the fountain so that it is clean enough to play in. However, it is still important to remind your kids to keep their mouths away from the water. Just like swimming-pool water, this is not drinking water! Meetings or gatherings of 25 people or more need to call ahead for a permit.

PHOTO BY JOE KENT

Washington Park

∧∧∧

FOGGY WITH SLEEP DEPRIVATION, my husband and I sat on a park bench in the warm sun and rocked our newborn. Butterflies floated to gentle landings on nearby blossoms, and our toddler paused in his manic race along curving garden paths to kneel and bury his nose in a flaming pink geranium. Then he sat up and beamed at us. Later, we watched bees dive into marigold hearts, and we gathered seeds from flowers whose petals had withered.

Tired of botanical pursuits, our family ambled over to the playground, full of bridges and slides and towers. The sleepy three of us settled in again as our little firecracker climbed and swung and ran with other kids.

Washington Park is 33 square blocks of lakes, lawns, trees, playgrounds, picnic tables, bicycle paths, jogging paths, soccer fields, tennis courts, fishing, horseshoe courts, a recreation center,

DENVER METRO CONVENTION & VISITORS BUREAU
PHOTO BY STAN OBERT

and abundant flower beds. Paths curve around and between the gardens and are perfect for strolling (or playing peek-a-boo, if you are 2½ years old).

If you wait until September to view the flower beds, they will be slightly past their prime, but the weather may be cooler. Also, many of the blossoms may be going to seed, and this is a good opportunity to show preschoolers how flowers repro-duce. Perhaps you can gather a few seeds in an old yogurt cup to take home and plant next spring.

The biggest drawback for us was the lack of convenient bathroom facilities (a challenge for those who are actively potty learning).

Washington Park is 33 square blocks of lakes, lawns, trees, playgrounds, picnic tables, bicycle paths, jogging paths, soccer fields, tennis courts, fishing, horseshoe courts, a recreation center, and abun-dant flower beds. Paths curve around and between the gar-dens and are perfect for strolling (or playing peek-a-boo if you are 2½ years old).

Sanitary facilities aside, Washington Park and its flower beds are perfect for a mellow, late summer outing. Next year we'll plan a picnic supper on the grass.

WHEN YOU GO:
Washington Park

Phone Number: 303/ 698-4930

Website: www.denvergov.org/content/template21232.asp

Directions: Washington Park takes up several blocks along Downing Street, between Virginia and Louisiana avenues. It is just a few blocks north of I-25 on Downing. The flower beds are on the west side of the park at about Ohio Avenue.

Season: The park is open year-round, but blooms peak in August and September

Hours: The park is open to the public 5 A.M. to 11 P.M. unless oth-erwise posted

Cost: Free

Facilities: One of the playgrounds is handicap accessible. Cement picnic tables are scattered around the park, and the trees offer nice shade. The closest bathroom to the flower beds is a San-o-let tucked under the trees where the park road crosses City Ditch. Otherwise, there are bathrooms in the Washington Park Recreation Center. They don't have diaper decks, but there is barely enough counter space to change a baby.

Special Considerations and Notes: Bring enough baby wipes to clean up grubby hands, because the only place to wash them is in the recreation center at one end of the park. Also, the flower beds are out in the open, so bring sun hats, plenty of sunscreen to protect young skin, and extra water to drink. On hot days, spray bottles of water add entertainment and a way to cool off youngsters.

∿∿

Washington Park and its flower beds are perfect for a mellow, late-summer outing.

∿∿

City Park

∧∧∧

CITY PARK IS THE QUEEN OF DENVER'S URBAN PLAZAS, and, appropriately, it sports a vast castle of a playground where kids hold court. Park benches, huge shade trees, picnic tables and expansive green lawns surround the jungle-gym-palace. Lavender tower roofs command the sky while swaying bridges cross wood-chip moats, below. On warm days, the structure is filled with shrieks and giggles as little citizens swarm through it. This is the largest playground in the City of Denver's system, and is a wildly popular destination.

The playground isn't the only thing that draws preschoolers to City Park. The area is also home to the Zoo, the Museum of Nature and Science, tennis courts, flower gardens, fountains, statues, summer concerts, and the Black Arts Festival. In warm months you can rent paddleboats and the park has been designated an IBA (important bird area) by the Audubon Society.

PHOTO BY JOE KENT

Additionally, the city's greenhouses, which grow all the flowers for the parks and parkways (over 330,000 plants) are located west of the zoo and are open for visits from the public.

With 314 acres, preschoolers (and their adults) find plenty of room for exploring, running, and just goofing around in City Park. It is truly a gem in Denver's crown.

WHEN YOU GO:
City Park

Phone Number: 303/ 331-4113
Website: www.denvergov.org/East_Denver_Parks
Address: 2100 Steel Street, Denver
Directions: Between York Street on the west and Colorado Boulevard on the east, the park stretches north from 17th Avenue to 26th Avenue. From I-25, take University Boulevard north past where it turns into Josephine Street and then into York Street. Turn into the park on 23rd Avenue. Or from I-70, take Colorado Boulevard south about 2 miles and turn west into the park on 23rd Avenue. The playground is southwest of the west entrance to the zoo.
Season: Open year-round
Hours: 5 A.M. to 11 P.M. unless otherwise posted
Cost: Free
Facilities: There are restrooms north of the playground, near the tennis courts, but they are often not open. Port-o-lets are available at various spots throughout the park.

PHOTO BY JOE KENT

Chapter 11

Potpourri

A LITTLE OF THIS, A LITTLE OF THAT

THROUGHOUT THE DENVER AREA there are all kinds of great places for preschoolers to visit that defy categories. So I threw a couple of our favorites into this catch-all chapter, called Potpourri. These places are terrific for broadening your kids' horizons, and hopefully they will inspire you to check out other sites where kids can see how the world works. Enjoy!

PHOTO BY JOE KENT

Enrichment Ideas:

1. When you visit a spot that sells them, buy a postcard or two while you are there. I usually let my kids pick out one each, and then I get them one that has a good overview shot of the whole place. Then find a box for your kids to decorate and store the postcards in. Encourage them to share their postcard collection often with as many different people as possible. It will help develop their memories and give them good practice using descriptive language—both important pre-reading skills.

2. Arthur's little sister D.W. wants to check out her own library books in D.W.'s *Library Card* by Marc Brown. In the process of getting the card and borrowing her first book, she learns important lessons that preschoolers can apply to many parts of their lives. *The Little Fire Engine* by Lois Lenski is an excellent pre-learning or follow-up book for a visit to the Firefighter's Museum. (But you will have to talk to your kids about getting out of a burning building immediately, leaving the sofas and lamps behind, contrary to what the book depicts. Still, this is a classic about Fireman Small.)

DENVER PUBLIC LIBRARY

The State Capitol

⋀⋀⋀

FROM CIVIC CENTER PARK, THE GLITTERING CAPITOL DOME towers into the blue Colorado sky. Red flagstone pathways angle through the park and converge at the base of granite stairs. Halfway up the steps an inscription reads, "one mile above sea level." We began to climb.

By the time we'd finished, we gazed down at Civic Center Park, 272 feet below, and a breeze wafted off the gold leaf cupola just above our heads. The view from the capitol's crown, as well as the clamber up the stairs, left us breathless.

Built from 1886 to 1908, the Colorado capitol's materials come from all over our state. The foundation is Fort Collins sandstone, and the outer walls are of Gunnison granite. The town of Marble provided marble for the interior stairs and floors, and Beulah provided beautiful rose onyx marble for wainscoting.

DENVER METRO CONVENTION & VISITORS BUREAU
PHOTO BY STAN OBERT

DENVER METRO CONVENTION & VISITORS BUREAU
PHOTO BY DAVID FALCONER

Cavernous halls, fancy bronze work, classical columns, beautiful murals, and stained glass combine to make this a truly grand public space, and it engenders a quiet, wide-eyed feeling. The nature of the legislature may be beyond a preschooler's grasp, but the architecture itself communicates that this is an important place where people do important work. Thinking about the governor or a state senator working in the capitol building will help kids to understand the significance of those individuals.

Amidst the grandiosity of the halls, familiar objects in the artwork are especially pleasing and comforting. For example, the elevator doors show bronze panels depicting a covered wagon, mining tools, a basket of apples, and other key parts of Colorado's history and economy. We enjoyed naming them and running our fingers over their shapes.

Cavernous halls, fancy bronze work, classical columns, beautiful murals, and stained glass combine to make this a truly grand public space.

A visit to the Colorado capitol isn't a long field trip, but it is impressive for young children, and it will provide them with a lasting memory of one of our state's most beautiful icons.

Phone Number: 303/ 866-2604

Website: www.state.co.us/gov_dir/leg_dir/lcsstaff/tourwelcome.htm

Address: 201 East Colfax, Denver

Directions: From I-25, take the Colfax Avenue exit and go east on Colfax Avenue about 1½ miles. The capitol building is between Lincoln and Grant streets on Colfax Avenue.

Season: All year, although closed on legal holidays except Martin Luther King Day and Presidents' Day

Hours: Open to the public, 9 A.M. to 5:30 P.M,. Monday through Friday, and on Saturdays, Memorial Day through Labor Day

Cost: Free

Facilities: Stroller and wheelchair accessible except for the 93 stairs up into the dome. Both men's and women's bathrooms are in the basement and have diaper decks. The cafeteria may be closed in the summer, although coffee and pop machines are available. There is a small gift shop.

Special Considerations and Notes: Guided tours are available to individuals and school groups, although they may be inappropriate for preschoolers. Young children often enjoy looking for figures in the streaks of the rose marble lining the foyer walls—more than 1,000 have been found, including the faces of George Washington and Molly Brown.

The stairs (93 in all) up into the dome are steep, winding, and very open. Small children are allowed up, but the climb is hard for them and dangerous. I only felt comfortable carrying my son all the way back down. Although the view from the top is spectacular, I don't recommend the trip unless you have a ratio of one adult to each child. A backpack carrier would be very helpful.

The Denver Public Library, Main Branch

∧∧∧

THE DENVER PUBLIC LIBRARY stands amidst Denver's most illustrious buildings, near the state capitol, next to the Denver Art Museum, and across from Civic Center Park. It strikes a commanding pose; its chunky roofline and toilet-paper-tube towers look like a giant preschooler's building-block creation. My 3-year-old was intrigued by the structure.

Inside, the library calls out for a tour. We rode the escalators and examined the murals that surround the main lobby. We checked out the periodicals room and the rows of file cabinets full of pictures. Although *I* thought we were there to go to the children's library, we ended up exploring the building first.

∧∧∧

In the rooms dedicated to young readers, the sheer number of books was almost overwhelming. It was hard to know where to start.

∧∧∧

Finally, in the rooms dedicated to young readers, the sheer number of books was almost overwhelming. It was hard to know where to start. We stumbled on a collection of musical CDs for children and brought home a couple of gems. We sat in Adirondack-style chairs, arranged in a semicircle, and gazed through tall windows at a giant chair sculpture on the outside lawn. A circus-tent motif and stuffed animals greeted us at every turn.

Eventually we found some books to borrow and made our way to the checkout desk for kids, located in the main lobby. It is built lower so little ones can watch what the librarian is doing.

∧∧∧

. . . its chunky roofline and toilet-paper-tube towers look like a giant preschoolers' building-block creation.

∧∧∧

Exploring the main branch of the Denver Public Library was a new twist on an old standby activity for our family. It was a wonderful diversion on a rainy day.

When You Go:
The Denver Public Library, Main Branch

Phone Number: 720/ 865-1111

Website: www.denver.lib.co.us

Address: 10 West 14th Avenue Parkway, Denver.

Directions: From I-25, take Colfax Avenue east to Broadway. Turn right (north) on Broadway and look for the library on the east side of the street between 13th and 14th avenues.

Season: Year-round, except for the following holidays: New Year's Day, Martin Luther King Day, Presidents' Day, Cesar Chavez Day (March 25), Easter, Memorial Day, Independence Day,

Labor Day, Veteran's Day, Thanksgiving, and Christmas Day. On the day before Thanksgiving, Christmas Eve, and New Year's Eve, the library closes at 4pm.

Hours: Monday, Tuesday, and Wednesday, 10 A.M. to 9 P.M.; Thursday, Friday, and Saturday, 10 A.M. to 5:30 P.M.; Sunday, 1 P.M. to 5 P.M.

Cost: Free

Facilities: The library is stroller and wheelchair accessible, and the bathrooms have diaper decks. In the children's library, the bathrooms have diminutive potties for the shortest patrons. Lunch is available in the Denver Art Museum, across the courtyard from the library. A small gift shop sells library-related items, and its hours are 10 A.M. to 5:30 P.M., Monday through Saturday, and 1 P.M. to 5 P.M. on Sunday.

Special Considerations: Tours of the children's library are available to preschool groups accompanied by a teacher. With a tour, you are likely to hear the story of the red-horse-on-the-chair sculpture, visible just outside the large windows. Schedule at least 4 weeks ahead and plan for at least one adult per group of 10 children, with a maximum group size of 25. For preschoolers unaffiliated with a school, a self-guided tour is available that includes activities and games with a map of the children's library. Also, librarians are happy to show kids and their parents around.

〰〰

Eventually we found some books to borrow and made our way to the checkout desk for kids, located in the main lobby. Exploring the main branch of the Denver Public Library was a new twist on an old standby activity for our family. It was a wonderful diversion on a rainy day.

〰〰

The Children's Museum of Denver

/W\

I SAT AT THE LUNCH COUNTER AND ORDERED A BURGER. Within seconds, the towheaded 3-year-old was handing me buns. After rummaging through drawers for a minute, he found the meat part and put that on the counter in front of me. Then he helped me sandwich it between the bread. After a pretend bite, I proclaimed my plastic burger "delicious!"

The Children's Museum of Denver is all about play. From the Center for the Young Child (a 3,700-square-foot playscape for children newborn to age 4) to the Assembly Plant (where older kids get hands-on experience with a variety of tools and recycled materials for building objects), the Children's Museum provides opportunities for kids to learn while playing.

PHOTO BY DIANE CLAUDE

At first glance, the place seemed busy and congested, full of nothing but toys. Initially, I was even a bit offended at the contrived, artificial feel of some of the exhibits. For instance, in the Center for the Young Child, there is a pretend "garden," in which the children can insert large carrots and beets into rows of square holes and then pull them out again. Couldn't kids learn about gardening, I thought, from a real garden more effectively?

ᐱᐱ

The Children's Museum of Denver is all about play. From the Center for the Young Child (a 3,700-square-foot playscape for children newborn to age 4) to the Assembly Plant (where older kids get hands-on experience with a variety of tools and recycled materials for building objects), the Children's Museum provides opportunities for kids to learn while playing.

ᐱᐱ

Perhaps. But kids can use play to come to terms with the reality of their world, and for that purpose, the toy garden was actually more useful than a real one. The vegetables in the play garden were "transplanted" many times and handled in ways that real ones could never tolerate.

With 9 different venues, each focusing on a different theme, the Children's Museum of Denver is too big to explore in one visit. Check out the website before visiting, or study the map of the building where you buy tickets, and decide which one or two areas you want to focus on. But be prepared to get sidetracked en route. Let your kids take the lead to pursue their own interests.

And be prepared to get sucked into their play. After all, the experience is always richer when shared with someone you love.

When You Go:
The Children's Museum of Denver

Phone Number: 303/ 433-7444 or 303/ 561-3370 for group reservations
Website: www.cmdenver.org
Address: 2121 Children's Museum Drive, Denver

Directions: From I-25, take the 23rd Avenue exit (exit #211) and go east to the first right on Children's Museum Drive. Follow the curved road to the green building with the purple pyramid on the top. Check the website for a map.

Season: Year-round except Thanksgiving, Christmas, New Year's, and Easter

Hours: Tuesday through Friday, 9 A.M. to 4 P.M.; Saturday, 10 A.M. to 5 P.M. Closed Mondays except Labor Day, Memorial Day, and school holidays.

Cost: Babies under one year old are free; ages 1–2 and seniors, 50 cents; ages 3–59, $6.50

Facilities: Wheelchairs can navigate through the museum, but strollers are not allowed in the playscapes. Stroller parking is available. Some of the bathrooms have short little potties and lower sinks, in addition to diaper decks. There is a small snack bar that is open for lunch and an area with tables (including kid-sized ones) if you want to bring your lunch or snack. On nice days, the patio with tables is also open. A gift shop sells a small assortment of toys and books.

∿∿

With 9 different venues, each focusing on a different theme, the Children's Museum of Denver is too big to explore in one visit. . . . Decide which one or two areas you want to focus on. But be prepared to get sidetracked en route. Let your kids take the lead to pursue their own interests. And be prepared to get sucked into their play.

∿∿

Denver Firefighters Museum

∧∨∧

EYES FLASHING LIKE EMERGENCY LIGHTS, the 4-year-old gripped the wheel and grinned, navigating imaginary streets on his way to a fire. His feet—clad in real fire boots—couldn't quite reach the pedals, and his red helmet kept slipping down over his face. No matter—he was on a mission, and nothing would stop him now!

Reaching his destination, he scrambled off the fire engine and climbed a platform to slide down a fireman's pole. At historic station number 1, now the Denver Firefighter's Museum, a kid's reverie can run like wildfire.

Built in 1909, the tall brick building was one the largest firehouses in Denver. It had two floors and covered nearly 11,000 square feet. Now the upstairs is devoted to hosting parties and events, while the main floor houses an impressive assembly of antique fire engines and historic artifacts from Denver's fire-fighting history. Almost all of the exhibits are hands-off, which can be a challenge for some preschoolers.

PHOTO BY JOE KENT

However, the kids are rewarded for good behavior when they get to the back of the museum, where there is a pile of boots, helmets, and coats in various sizes for dressing up.

The museum even has a box of authentic masks with hoses attached to make the outfits complete.

A TV is set up for watching fire-safety videos from wooden benches. The museum offers one with Sparky the Fire Dog for 2- and 3-year-olds, and "Get Low and Go" for kids 4 and up.

PHOTO BY JOE KENT

Then it's time to climb on the fire truck. The only vehicle in the museum that visitors are allowed to touch, it is a beauty. A 1926 American LaFrance Pumper, it has lots of knobs and dials and levers. A huge black steering wheel lords over chrome headlights and a big brass bell. Benches in the truck's rear carried a fire crew and will still accommodate at least a dozen young rescue heroes. Hoses and a hook and ladder are on board and at the ready.

The Denver Firefighter's Museum combines a number of surefire elements for a good time: big trucks, uniforms, heroism, something to climb on. It's a preschooler's dream come true.

WHEN YOU GO:
Denver Firefighters Museum

Phone Number: 303/ 892-1436
Website: www.firedenver.org
Address: 1326 Tremont Place, Denver
Directions: From I-25, take the Colfax Avenue exit and go east into downtown Denver. Turn left (northeast) on Welton, then right on 14th Street, and right again on Tremont Place. The

museum is in a tall, thin, antique brick building. Check the website for a map.

Season: Year-round

Hours: Monday through Saturday, 10 A.M. to 2 P.M.

Cost: $3.00 for adults, $2.00 for seniors and kids

Facilities: Strollers and wheelchairs can navigate through the first floor of the museum. A gift shop sells a small assortment of toys and books, mostly related to firefighters. No food is permitted in the museum.

Special Considerations: Call ahead for tour information and to schedule birthday parties.

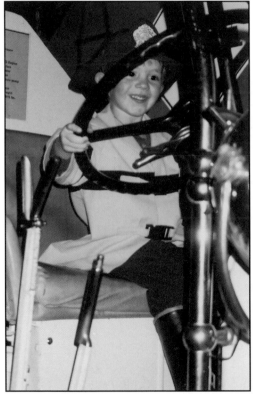

PHOTO BY JOE KENT

About the Author

ᐱᐱ

CAROLYN SUTTON is a Denver native, a freelance travel writer, and the mom of two preschoolers. Before getting married and having babies, she received a diploma in education from the University of Colorado in Boulder and taught junior-high and high-school science. Now she writes about the adventures she and her husband have, traveling with their little ones.

Publisher's Note:

Colorado's Ocean Journey Aquarium

ᐱᐱ

AT THE TIME THIS BOOK WENT TO PRESS, Colorado's Ocean Journey Aquarium's future was very much in question. Headlines had already proclaimed the aquarium's sinking and it had funds to operate for only a few months. Sadly, we pulled the piece on Ocean Journey.

If by good fortune Colorado's Ocean Journey is still open when you pick up this book, by all means plan a visit with your preschoolers! Many of its most loyal patrons are under 3½ feet tall for good reason.

Its two main exhibits trace the Colorado and Kampar Rivers from mountaintop to seashore. Visitors can feel and smell the climates the waters pass through in addition to meeting the wildlife living on the banks and below the surfaces. For entertainment and education of very young children, the value is there.

It is our sincere hope that in future editions we will return Colorado's Ocean Journey to its rightful place among the best outings for kids under 6 years old.

What People Are Saying about
The Preschooler's Guide to Denver

∧∧∧

How many times have we gone to the same place twice because we couldn't think of something new? **The Preschooler's Guide to Denver** *gave me lots of new ideas about places to take my kids!*
　　　　　　　—Susan Strobel Maly, RN, Mother of 2 Preschoolers

This book makes it so easy.
　　　　　　　—Laura Hargrave, Product Manager, Mother of 2 preschoolers

I think the book is incredibly helpful... I liked the "When You Go" sections best. I felt like we were always doing the same things. This book has become a major source of reference in our home... together we plan something to do and see each week that is new and different!
　　　　　　　—Ann Coyhis, Retired Elementary School Teacher,
　　　　　　　　　　　　　　　Mother of 3 preschoolers

This is a great resource for parents with young children. Best were the catchy subtitles, creative ideas, and lots of information regarding each activity. It would be a great gift for someone moving into the neighborhood with small children.
　　　　　　　—Stephanie Power, Special Education Teacher, Mother of 5

This book would benefit me as I have plenty of grandchildren to entertain and it's good to have one place to look up all the information. What's best about the book is the writing and the incredible information.
　　　—Mary Cella, Director of St. Mary's Academy Early Learning Center

Could I order a case? This book would make a great two-year-old birthday gift or shower gift for that matter!